Lexcel Small Practi

Related titles from Law Society Publishing:

Anti-Money Laundering Toolkit
Alison Matthews

COFAs Toolkit
Jeremy Black and Florence Perret du Cray

COLPs Toolkit
Michelle Garlick

Equality and Diversity Toolkit
Mark Lomas

Lexcel Business Continuity Planning Toolkit
The Law Society

Lexcel Client Care Toolkit (2nd edn)
The Law Society

Lexcel Financial Management and Business Planning Toolkit
The Law Society

Lexcel Information Management Toolkit
The Law Society

Lexcel People Management Toolkit
The Law Society

Lexcel Risk Management Toolkit (2nd edn)
The Law Society

All books from Law Society Publishing can be ordered through good bookshops or direct from our distributors, Prolog, by telephone 0870 850 1422 or email **lawsociety@prolog.uk.com**. Please confirm the price before ordering.

For further information or a catalogue, please contact our editorial and marketing office by email **publishing@lawsociety.org.uk**.

Lexcel Small Practice Toolkit

The Law Society

The Law Society

ISBN 978-1-907698-42-2

Crown copyright material in Annexes 1D and 1E is reproduced with the permission of the Controller of Her Majesty's Stationery Office.

Published in 2013 by the Law Society
113 Chancery Lane, London WC2A 1PL

Typeset by Columns Design XML Ltd, Reading
Printed by TJ International Ltd, Padstow, Cornwall

The paper used for the text pages of this book is FSC® certified. FSC (the Forest Stewardship Council®) is an international network to promote responsible management of the world's forests.

FSC
www.fsc.org
MIX
Paper from
responsible sources
FSC® C013056

Contents

Preface

Since the introduction of outcomes-focused regulation and increasing demand from stakeholders, there has never been a more important time for firms of all sizes to consider implementing Lexcel. The standard has been created for solicitors, by solicitors and continues to be the only quality standard solely for legal practices. Lexcel v5 provides practices of all sizes with a framework to manage their businesses in accordance with best practice principles.

This toolkit has been created to assist smaller firms in creating the necessary policies, plans and procedures in order to achieve Lexcel accreditation. The practical templates and supporting text allow firms to understand what is required and should be used as a starting point for the creation of your firm's own procedures.

The Lexcel office would like to thank Bob Partridge of PDA for his contribution to the toolkit. We would also like to thank Clare Jarratt and Simon Blackett for their continued support creating the entire Lexcel toolkit series.

We would also like to thank AWB Charlesworth Solicitors, Breeze and Wyles LLP, Lesley Scott, Michelmores LLP, Nockolds Solicitors Ltd, Petherbridge Bassra Solicitors and Wilsons LLP.

Lexcel Office
The Law Society

About this toolkit

Format

The chapters have been placed in order of the eight sections of the Lexcel standard:

Section 1 – Structures and policies
Section 2 – Strategic plans
Section 3 – Financial management
Section 4 – Information management
Section 5 – People management
Section 6 – Risk management
Section 7 – Client care
Section 8 – File and case management

Definitions

Manual – the term refers to the manuals (electronic or hard copy) that a practice has created which combine the key policies, plans and procedures related to the management of the business. Alternative names used include operational, quality or office procedures manual.

Policy – this is a general approach taken within the practice to the issue in question. A policy defines why a particular approach is adopted by the practice. All policies must have a named person who is responsible for their implementation and a procedure to ensure that they are reviewed.

Procedure – this is a written description of how an activity will occur within a practice. A procedure describes the steps that staff should follow in order to complete an activity. There is an increasing tendency for procedures to be documented in a more descriptive style, e.g. 'This policy will be reviewed annually by the COLP'. A more traditional way is to be more prescriptive, for example, 'This policy will be reviewed annually by the COLP through examinations of the data presented by Heads of Department'. It is for each practice to decide how detailed it wants its procedures to be, but they should always be easy for people to find, understand and implement.

Plan – this is an outline of where a practice desires to be in the future and describes how it intends to arrive at that destination. In general, practices should develop plans in the manner and detail that they consider appropriate, assuming a basic level of adequacy. The format of plans is a matter for individual practices.

Using this toolkit

This toolkit contains template policies, procedures and plans which are provided in a Microsoft Word format to enable individual practices to tailor them to their specific requirements. In a number of instances, practices will need to insert information into the templates, and guidance is provided where this is the case. In certain documents, alternative paragraphs are provided to enable practices to make choices that are appropriate to them.

Specific documents provide prompts for the issues that should be considered when inserting relevant content. In a small number of instances, detailed guidelines are provided for the completion of the documents.

1 Structures and policies

1.1 Documentation

1.1 Practices will have documentation setting out the:

    a: legal framework under which they operate

    b: management structure which designates the responsibilities of individuals and their accountability.

Practices should document the legal framework under which they operate to ensure there is clarity on the type of business for employees, stakeholders and clients. This can be as simple as a statement indicating whether a practice is an LLP, limited company, partnership, or simply defaults to the Partnership Act 1890.

The management and supervision structure should also be clear. This can be provided by a brief description of it, together with organisation charts. These charts could also be used to highlight the supervision structure within the practice while satisfying any requirements to have a named supervisor for each area of work within the practice.

1.2 Risk management

1.2 Practices will have a risk management policy, which must include:

    a: strategic risk

    b: operational risk

    c: regulatory risk

    d: the person responsible for the policy

    e: a procedure for an annual review of the policy, to verify it is in effective operation across the practice.

1.2.1 Overview

Practices should be clear about their approach to risk management. Risk management should:

- be integral to strategic planning and review;
- be embedded in the practice's culture;
- be set out in a clearly defined policy;
- permeate the whole organisation through its policies and procedures.

1.2.2 Context

Risk management should not be viewed in isolation. It must be looked at in the context of everything a practice does: its strategic aims and objectives, its culture and the way it operates. A fundamental question that practices should ask is: 'What could prevent us from achieving our objectives?'

Risks identified in answer to this question will provide a compelling case for ensuring that risk management is an integral part of strategic planning. Deployed effectively, risk management can support the achievement of aims and objectives such as:

- running a profitable business (private practices);
- delivering cost-effective services (in-house departments);
- providing high quality legal advice;
- providing high levels of client service;
- complying with regulatory and legislative requirements.

1.2.3 Types of risk

Risks tend to be split into three categories:

- *Strategic risk* – events and their consequences that could affect the viability or success of your practice are strategic risks, although a catastrophic operational risk (such as a negligence claim that exceeds your level of professional indemnity insurance cover) could be seen as strategic risks. These types of risks are often triggered by external factors such as the economy or catastrophic events.
- *Operational risk* – events and their consequences that arise from day-to-day business activities are operational risks. For example, a lack of consistent, rigorous procedures relating to the start, progress and conclusion of matters would expose your practice to the risk of complaints and indemnity claims. Some operational risks can become strategic risks if action is not taken to address them. For example, aside from any regulatory implications, continued inconsistent application of client care requirements could result in significant loss of business and compromise the viability of the practice.
- *Regulatory risk* – acts or omissions that could give rise to regulatory consequences are regulatory risks. See **1.3–1.5** for examples of a number of regulatory risks affecting law firms in England and Wales.

A risk management policy is given at **Annex 1A**.

1.3 Outsourcing

1.3 Practices will have a policy in relation to outsourced activities, which must include:

   a: details of all outsourced activities
   b: procedures to check the quality of outsourced work

   c: steps to ensure providers have taken appropriate precautions to ensure information will be protected
   d: a list of all providers of services
   e: the person responsible for the policy
   f: a procedure for an annual review of the policy, to verify it is in effective operation across the practice

A 'legal activity' is defined in s.12 of the Legal Services Act 2007, and includes reserved legal activities (which include the exercise of a right of audience; the conduct of litigation; reserved instrument activities (key elements of conveyancing); probate activities (limited to the application and grant); notarial activities and the administration of oaths); and also includes the provision of legal advice or assistance, or representation, in connection with the application of the law, or with any form of resolution of legal disputes.

Outsourcing is increasingly being considered by practices as a way of reducing costs while maintaining a full quality service to clients. Activities to consider are those where a practice uses a third party to undertake work that the practice would normally do itself, and where the practice remains responsible for the work. The use of counsel and experts does not normally come within the scope of outsourcing. Practices must include these if the work is activities they would normally do. For best practice, any external service providers should be included.

Activities that could constitute outsourcing include:

* activities which would normally be undertaken by a paralegal;
* initial drafting of contracts;
* legal secretarial services – digital dictation to an outsourced secretarial service for word processing or typing;
* proofreading;
* research;
* document review;
* Companies House filing;
* due diligence, for example in connection with the purchase of a company;
* IT functions which support the delivery of legal activities;
* business process outsourcing.

An outsourcing policy is given at **Annex 1B**.

1.4 Equality and diversity

1.4 Practices will have a policy on the avoidance of discrimination and the promotion of equality and diversity, which must include:

   a: employment and partnership, recruitment and selection, training and conditions of service and promotions within the practice
   b: the delivery of service
   c: the instruction of counsel and experts in all professional dealings
   d: a procedure to deal with complaints and disciplinary issues in breach of the policy

e: a procedure to monitor diversity
f: training of all personnel on compliance with equality and diversity requirements
g: the person responsible for the policy
h: a procedure for an annual review of the policy, to verify it is in effective operation across the practice.

The Lexcel standard has increased its requirements for equality and diversity, in line with the SRA Handbook. The main areas of extension from previous versions of the Lexcel standard are the need to:

• include details of the arrangements that have been made to ensure that training on the subject is delivered to all staff;
• describe how diversity is monitored throughout the practice;
• describe how complaints relating to breaches of the policy are dealt with.

An equality and diversity policy is given at **Annex 1C**.

1.5 Health and safety at work

1.5 Practices will have a policy in relation to the health and safety of all personnel and visitors to the practice, which must include:

a: the person responsible for the policy
b: a procedure for an annual review of the policy, to verify it is in effective operation across the practice.

Health and safety is a subject that carries legislative responsibilities for all organisations, within (the list is not exhaustive):

• Health and Safety at Work etc Act 1974.
• Workplace (Health, Safety and Welfare) Regulations 1992, SI 1992/3004.
• Health and Safety (Display Screen Equipment) Regulations 1992, SI 1992/279.
• Control of Substances Hazardous to Health Regulations (COSHH) 2002, SI 2002/2677 (as amended).
• Management of Health and Safety at Work Regulations 1999, SI 1999/3242.
• Manual Handling Operations Regulations 1992, SI 1992/2793 (as amended in 2002).
• Health and Safety (First-Aid) Regulations 1981, SI 1981/917 and associated Approved Code of Practice 1997.

1.5.1 Basic summary of requirements

• Every organisation must conduct assessments of the health and safety risks that exist both within its premises and in the nature of the work that it undertakes. Following these assessments, the organisation is required to decide on appropriate levels of training of staff and equipment that it supplies. If the organisation has more than five employees, it must record the outcome of its health and safety risk assessment.

- Every organisation that employs more than five people must have a health and safety policy.
- There is a duty to consult employees on health and safety issues. This can be done in a number of ways including listening and talking to them about:

  - health and safety and the work they do;
  - how risks are controlled;
  - the best ways of providing information and training.

- Under normal circumstances, the work undertaken by law practices would probably be considered to be of low risk although there could be exceptions if, for example, home visits are conducted in areas that may be deemed risky, or with clients whose conduct could be unstable/aggressive/in any other way risky.
- The Health and Safety (First-Aid) Regulations 1981 and associated Approved Code of Practice 1997 deal with the first-aid requirements that organisations must observe.

There is no mandatory requirement for an organisation to have trained first-aiders in the workplace, but there is a requirement to have at least one person appointed to take charge of first-aid arrangements, which includes looking after the first-aid equipment and facilities and calling emergency services when required.

1.5.2 Sources of help

The Health and Safety Executive website (**www.hse.gov.uk**) contains many downloadable and free publications which contain useful guidance and templates for the management of health and safety. The links to some of them are provided below.

- Health and safety made simple **www.hse.gov.uk/pubns/indg449.pdf**
- Health and Safety Law – what you need to know **www.hse.gov.uk/pubns/law.pdf**
- Working with VDUs **www.hse.gov.uk/pubns/indg36.pdf**
- Five steps to risk assessment **www.hse.gov.uk/pubns/indg163.pdf**
- First aid at work **www.hse.gov.uk/pubns/priced/l74.pdf**

A template for a health and safety policy can be found at **Annex 1D** and a risk assessment template at **Annex 1E**.

A central policy, plan and procedure register, allowing for the recording and review of all of a practice's policies, plans and procedures, can be found at **Annex 1F**.

1.6 Corporate social responsibility (CSR)

1.6 Practices should have a policy in relation to community and social responsibility, which must include:

a: the person responsible for the policy

b: a procedure for an annual review of the policy, to verify it is in effective operation across the practice.

There is evidence that when practices are tendering for the provision of legal services to organisations, they are sometimes asked to produce their corporate social responsibility (CSR) policies.

There are many areas that could be covered by such a policy, but common ones include (the list is not exhaustive):

- responsible disposal of waste materials, e.g. printer and toner cartridges;
- reducing electricity use;
- car sharing initiatives;
- cycle purchasing initiatives;
- sponsorship of local sports clubs, schools, etc.;
- pro bono work for charities, voluntary and community projects;
- voluntary work by staff in the community, e.g. assisting with reading in schools in deprived areas;
- methods for conserving water and electricity during normal operations;
- offering work experience to young people from disadvantaged backgrounds.

Other examples of what can be included in such a policy can be found in guidance to assessors of the Business Excellence Model (EFQM), details of which can be found at **http://www.bqf.org.uk/**

ISO 26000 is an international standard relating to social responsibility. More information can be found at **www.iso.org/sr**

Annex 1A
Risk management policy

Commitment

[*Name of practice*] is committed to running the business in accordance with proper corporate governance and sound financial and risk management principles. Risk management is an integral part of our strategic planning and review processes and underpins all our policies and procedures.

Scope

This policy affects all permanent and temporary employees, and all systems or processes for the identification, control and monitoring of risks. More particularly, it covers the following categories of risk:

- Strategic risk [*identify what you understand by strategic risk, giving examples relevant to your practice*]
- Operational risk [*identify what you understand by operational risk, giving examples relevant to your practice*]
- Regulatory risk [*identify what you understand by regulatory risk, giving examples relevant to your practice*]

Approach

The practice has initiated a systematic approach to the management of risk including:

- ensuring that the office manual is fully compliant with the Lexcel standard;
- compiling a risk register;
- maintaining a list of work that the practice will and will not undertake;
- conducting an annual review of claims and complaints data;
- providing staff briefing and training on risk identification, management and review.

Responsibilities

Risk manager

The designated risk manager for the practice is [*name*]. [He/she] has overall responsibility for risk management in the practice and [is also/reports to] the practice's compliance officer for legal practice (COLP).

[Senior management team/sole practitioner name]

[Senior management team/sole practitioner name] is responsible for determining the strategic direction of the practice and for carrying out strategic risk reviews. They are also responsible for creating the culture and environment for risk management to operate effectively throughout the practice.

Supervisors

Supervisors have primary responsibility for managing operational and regulatory risks on a day-to-day basis. They are also responsible for promoting risk awareness within their teams.

Staff

All staff are responsible for identifying risks and reporting risk issues at a level appropriate to their role so that supervisors can ensure that the necessary controls are in place. In order to facilitate this, all staff are required to keep up to date with the policies and procedures in the office manual.

Review

In order to ensure that it remains fit for purpose, this policy will be formally reviewed at least annually by *[senior management team/sole practitioner name]*. This review process will also serve as a means of continually improving the practice's approach to risk management.

Signed:

[Name]

Risk manager

Date:

Annex 1B

Outsourcing policy

[*Name of practice*] recognises that the use of outsourcing can assist in the provision of cost effective, high quality services for clients, while acknowledging that any use of outsourced services must comply with the regulatory requirements that are outlined below.

It is the policy of the practice to maintain constant awareness of outsourcing needs that may arise, and to ensure that any external services that are used are supervised to maintain the best possible service to clients. This document contains:

(a) regulatory requirements and guidance relating to outsourcing;
(b) the general principles that the practice will apply to outsourcing; and
(c) the procedures that will be followed at all times in order to maintain these principles and achieve these objectives.

Scope

The application of this policy applies to all individuals working at all levels and grades, including partners, senior managers, officers, directors, employees, consultants, contractors, trainees, home workers, part-time and fixed-term employees, casual and agency staff and volunteers, collectively referred to as staff in this policy.

General principles applied by the practice

1. Clients will be told at the beginning of each matter that the practice may at some stage during the conduct of the matter consider outsourcing work related to the matter.
2. If a decision is taken to outsource work relating to a matter, the permission of the client will be sought beforehand.
3. Where outsourcing is used in a matter the fee earner and matter supervisor are responsible for ensuring that the highest quality of work is maintained.
4. Where outsourcing is used in a matter the fee earner and matter supervisor are responsible for ensuring that client property and documents remain secure at all times.
5. Reserved legal activity or immigration work will only be outsourced to individuals who are sufficiently qualified, competent, and where appropriate, adequately supervised.

The practice's outsourcing conditions

Any proposal to outsource legal activities or operational functions critical to the delivery of any legal activities must receive written approval from [*name of person that must provide this approval*].

Prior to agreeing services with any external provider, the practice will ensure that the following conditions have been met:

1. [*Name*] has conducted due diligence enquiries about the proposed contractor ('contractor'), and is satisfied, and can if required produce evidence upon which this satisfaction is based, that the contractor is a reputable organisation, properly constituted as a business, and has the resources to undertake the outsourced work in a manner consistent with the practice's policy of ensuring maximum quality and confidentiality of service and advice to its clients.

2. [*Name*] will confirm that [he/she] has seen and read the contractor's business continuity/disaster recovery plan, and is satisfied that, if implemented, it would result in the contractor being able to fulfil its outsourcing commitments in the event of an emergency or disaster occurring.

3. [*Name*] will confirm that [he/she] has seen and read the contractor's equality and diversity and health and safety policies, and that [he/she] is satisfied that they comply with the current UK legal and regulatory requirements that apply at any time.

4. The contractor has in place a confidentiality policy that [*name*] has seen and is satisfied will, if implemented, ensure that all client matters will remain confidential.

5. [*Name*] is satisfied that the confidentiality policy has been explained to all of the contractor's employees.

6. The contractor has in place a conflicts of interests policy that [*name*] has seen and is satisfied will, if strictly implemented, ensure that all conflicts of interests that exist or may in the future exist at any time with the contractor or the contractor's employees, can be identified and addressed.

7. [*Name*] is satisfied that all contracted and subcontracted employees of the contractor have received thorough training, both initial and ongoing, on the contractor's conflicts of interests policy and identifying and dealing with conflicts of interests.

8. [*Name*] is satisfied that the contractor has procedures and facilities to ensure that any document or property belonging to the client which is handed to the contractor, will be kept secure from risks such as fire, theft or water ingress, and can be readily identified and retrieved.

9. [*Name*] is satisfied that the people employed by the contractor to undertake the outsourced work:

    (a) have the necessary qualifications and experience to deal with the work, and in the case of a reserved legal activity, are authorised to do so;
    (b) are adequately supervised by someone with the appropriate qualifications and experience; and
    (c) should there be a change of individual(s) who is/are undertaking the outsourced work, the contractor will immediately inform [*name*], providing full details including the names, status and qualifications of the new or additional staff.

10. The agreement with the contractor is in writing and will be made available at all times upon request by the SRA and [*name of practice*]. It will also stipulate that the contractor will agree to provide any information requested by the SRA and [*name of practice*].

11. The agreement with the contractor allows that the SRA and [*name of practice*] can visit the contractor's premises for their regulatory and monitoring purposes.

Risk assessments

If it is decided to outsource a substantial amount of work within a matter to a contractor, then the fee earner must conduct and record an assessment of the risk contained within the matter, and this must be countersigned by the matter supervisor, or, if the fee earner is self supervising, by [*name*].

Quality checking

Fee earners and, where appropriate, supervisors who have outsourced work to contractors will, on every occasion that work is outsourced, check to ensure that the work received from the contractors fully complies with the original briefing, including agreed timescales. A 'monitoring of outsourced work form' will be completed on every occasion, unless the outsourced work is of a regular and similar nature, e.g. typing/word processing, or the provision of IT services.

If the outsourcing comprises regular and similar types of work such as those indicated above, every piece of work, including routine letters, which has been so undertaken will be thoroughly checked before it is sent to the client. In the case of work of a regular and similar nature, the supervisor of the team for whom the work is undertaken will complete a 'monitoring of outsourced work form' every [*calendar month/quarter/biannually*].

Each head of department will retain a record of these monitoring forms, and will review them every three months and report to [*name of body or person that has approved the outsourcing*] any patterns of inadequate or poor quality work or service from any contractor.

Corrective/remedial actions

Any outsourced work that is found to be inadequate for whatever reason will be returned to the contractor, with clear instructions for corrective or remedial action that must be done in order to correct or remedy the work, together with a clear timescale within which the work must be completed and returned.

Where there is a need for corrective or remedial action, unless there are unusual and extenuating circumstances, the practice will not accept any charge for this work from the contractor.

In circumstances where a pattern of inadequate or poor quality work or service is being consistently received from a contractor, a report will be submitted to [*name*].

If it is deemed necessary, meetings will take place with the contractor concerned with a view to ensuring an improvement in future work. The practice will always retain the option of immediately terminating any outsourcing contract.

Record keeping

The compliance officer for legal practice (COLP) will maintain a record of all outsourced activities and providers for a period of five years following the cessation of individual outsourcing agreements.

Current suppliers

There is a list of services that are currently outsourced, together with details of those who are providing these services at the end of this policy.

Responsibility and review

The person responsible for the maintenance and review of this policy is [*name*].

[*Name*] will review this policy at least [annually/biannually/quarterly], making any amendments that are required, and report to the [partnership/management board/ executive].

Outsourced activities

Supplier	Outsourced activity	Other comments

Outsourcing monitoring	
Supplier of outsourced work	
Reviewer	
Date of review	
Work reviewed	
Comments on work reviewed	
Did work meet required standard?	Yes ☐ No ☐
Actions required or undertaken following review	
Signature of reviewer	

Annex 1C
Equality and diversity policy

Policy statement

[*Name of practice*] is committed to eliminating unlawful discrimination, harassment and bullying, and to promoting equality and diversity within our policies, practices and procedures. We are also committed to promoting equality and diversity in the practice. This applies to our professional dealings with clients, staff and partners, other solicitors and any third parties. We shall treat everyone appropriately and with the same attention, courtesy and respect regardless of:

(a) age;
(b) disability;
(c) gender reassignment;
(d) race;
(e) nationality, colour, ethnic or national origins;
(f) religion;
(g) gender;
(h) sexual orientation;
(i) marital status/civil partnership;
(j) Aids/HIV positive status;
(k) pregnancy, maternity, paternity or caring responsibility;
(l) work pattern;
(m) membership or non-membership of a trade union; or
(n) any other reason which is irrelevant to the employee's ability to do the job.

The practice will take all reasonable steps to ensure that employees do not unlawfully discriminate under the terms of this policy and any legislation in force.

Scope

This policy covers all individuals working at all levels and grades, including partners, senior managers, officers, directors, employees, consultants, contractors, trainees, home workers, part-time and fixed-term employees, casual and agency staff and volunteers, collectively referred to as staff in this policy.

Third parties who have access to the practice's electronic communication systems and equipment are also required to comply with this policy.

Implementation

Ultimate responsibility for implementing the policy rests with [*name*]. The partners have appointed [*name*] to be responsible for the operation of the policy. All employees and partners are expected to pay due regard to the provisions of this policy and are responsible for ensuring compliance with it when undertaking their jobs or representing the practice.

Meeting client needs

As a provider of private and publicly funded legal services, the practice will treat all clients equally and fairly and not unlawfully discriminate against them. The practice will also take steps to promote equality of opportunity in relation to access to the legal services that we provide, taking account of the diversity of the communities that we serve.

The practice is committed to meeting the diverse needs of clients, and will take steps to identify the needs of clients in our community, and develop policies and procedures setting out how we will meet clients' needs and for ensuring the services we provide are accessible to all. We will take account, in particular, of the needs of clients with a disability, and clients who are unable to communicate effectively in English. We will consider whether particular groups are predominant within our client base and devise appropriate policies to meet their needs.

The practice will devise policies and procedures to promote and raise awareness to ensure that our services are accessible for a diverse range of clients.

In particular we will:

(a) in the development of our policies, take account of the interests of all sections of society;
(b) ensure that, wherever possible, the services we provide meet the needs and expectations of all our clients;
(c) seek to influence others with whom we often work, and from whom we purchase goods and services, to share our commitment to valuing the diversity of our society;
(d) regularly assess our progress towards becoming a diverse organisation providing excellent service to all sections of society;
(e) organise training to ensure that all members of staff are aware of the need to understand the purpose of the policy and to put the policy into practice;
(f) ensure all new and existing employees are referred to the equality and diversity policy;
(g) ensure that partners and employees:

   (i)   deal with people with courtesy, politeness and consideration regardless of background;
   (ii)   take care to assess what clients can understand and to ask clients how they need to communicate – rather than make assumptions about this based on their ethnic origin, age or disability;
   (iii) ensure that clients are advised that, where the office premises are not accessible to them, a home visit can be arranged;
   (iv)   in the case of clients with a physical disability visiting the office premises, ensure that, as far as possible, their safety is assured and access to the premises is organised;
   (v)   provide clients with an impairment (visual, hearing, or speech) with options for communication;
   (vi)   in a case of clients where English is not their first language, provide access to language interpretations/translation wherever possible.

Dealing with third parties

The practice will not unlawfully discriminate in dealings with third parties. This applies to dealings with other legal service providers, e.g. counsel and general procurement, medical, mechanical and other experts that may be appointed to provide specialist services and advice.

The practice will instruct third parties on the basis of their skills, experience and ability, and not unlawfully discriminate, or encourage others to unlawfully discriminate, on the grounds of their age, gender, marital status, race, religion, sexual orientation or disability.

Employment

As an employer, the practice will treat all staff (as described under 'Scope' above) and job applicants fairly, and not unlawfully discriminate against them. This applies equally to voluntary positions and anyone undertaking work experience with the practice. This will, for example, include arrangements for recruitment and selection, terms and conditions of employment, access to training opportunities, access to promotion and transfers, grievance and disciplinary processes, demotions, selection for redundancies, dress code, references, bonus schemes, work allocation and any other employment related activities.

The practice recognises the benefits of having a diverse work force and will take steps to ensure that:

(a) it endeavours to recruit from the widest practical pool of qualified candidates;
(b) employment opportunities are open and accessible to all on the basis of their individual qualities and personal merit, while at the same time, applying a standard skills requirement;
(c) where appropriate, positive action measures are taken to attract applicants from all sections of society;
(d) all recruitment agencies acting for the practice are made aware of the practice's equality and diversity policy and are expected to work within it;
(e) each member of staff is guaranteed a contract of employment;
(f) it commits to a grievance and disciplinary procedure as part of a 'dignity at work programme'.

The practice will treat all employees appropriately, and create a working environment which is free from unlawful discrimination, and one which respects the diverse backgrounds and beliefs of employees. The provision of benefits such as flexible working hours, maternity and other leave arrangements, performance appraisal systems, dress code, bonus schemes and any other conditions of employment, will not unlawfully discriminate against any employee on the grounds of age, gender and gender reassignment, marital status, race, religion or belief, sexual orientation and disability.

Where appropriate and necessary, the practice will endeavour to provide appropriate facilities and conditions of service which take into account the specific needs of employees arising from, for example, their disability, ethnic or cultural background, gender and gender reassignment, responsibilities as carers, religion or belief or sexual orientation.

Promotion within the practice (including to partnership) will be made without reference to any of the forbidden grounds, and will be based solely on merit. The selection criteria and processes for recruitment and promotion will be kept under review to ensure that there is no unjustifiably discriminating impact on any particular group.

While positive action measures may be taken in accordance with relevant anti-discrimination legislation, to encourage applications from underrepresented groups, appointments to all jobs will be based solely on merit. All employees will have equal access to training and other career development opportunities appropriate to their experience and abilities. However, the practice will take appropriate positive action measures to provide special training support for groups which are underrepresented in the work force, and encourage them to take up training and career development opportunities.

Where partners or employees choose to disclose information regarding their sexual orientation or religion, steps will be taken to ensure that they are not being discriminated in any respect. The practice is aware that individuals may choose not to disclose this information, and that care will be taken to avoid discrimination in such cases.

Contravention of this policy

Proven acts of unlawful discrimination on any of the forbidden grounds, by employees or partners of the practice, will result in disciplinary action, as will any failure to comply with this policy.

The practice will take appropriate action on receipt of any complaint of unlawful discrimination on any of the forbidden grounds that is made by employees, partners, clients or third parties. Any complaints of unlawful discrimination could, if upheld, be treated as gross misconduct, with the attendant consequences.

Complaints procedure

Anyone who feels that they have been subjected to a breach or breaches of this policy should immediately inform [name]. [Name] will deal with the complaint in accordance with the practice's grievance procedures, and if necessary, invoke the practice's disciplinary procedures.

All complaints and reported incidents will be thoroughly investigated, and the complainant will be informed of the outcome.

[Name] will monitor the number and outcome of complaints of discrimination made by employees, clients, partners and any third party, and a record will be kept.

Monitoring equality and diversity

The practice will store equality and diversity data as confidential personal data, and restrict access to this information. Equality and diversity information will be used exclusively for the purpose of equality and diversity monitoring, and have no bearing on opportunities or benefits. The elements to be monitored are:

(a) the recruitment and selection process (applicants and existing staff and partners);
(b) promotion and transfer;
(c) all training;
(d) terms and conditions of employment;
(e) work life balance policies, e.g. flexible working requests;
(f) grievance and disciplinary procedures;
(g) resignations, redundancies and dismissals.

With regard to personnel and clients, the practice will provide equality and diversity information required by the Solicitors Regulation Authority and [name(s) of other organisations if applicable, e.g Legal Aid Agency].

Training

[Name] will identify equality and diversity training needs for individuals and/or the practice, and draw up a plan to address these as appropriate.

Equality and diversity training is one of the core generic subjects that will be delivered to everyone in the practice, and it is anticipated that this training will take place at least every two years, or more frequently should any issues of concern arise, or major regulatory and/or legislative changes occur.

Policy monitoring and review

[Name] will review the operation of this policy annually (or more regularly if any non-compliance or problems concerning equality and diversity issues with clients or personnel arise). The practice will take remedial action if any non-compliance with this policy is discovered, or if barriers to equality and diversity become apparent. When reviewing the policy, [name] will consider the outcome of monitoring and review activities and the training plan.

Annex 1D

Health and safety policy

This is the statement of general policy and arrangements for:	*[Name of practice]*		
Overall and final responsibility for health and safety is that of:	*[Name]*		
Day-to-day responsibility for ensuring this policy is put into practice is delegated to:	*[Name]*		
Statement of general policy	**Name of person responsible**	**Action/ Arrangements** *[Customise to meet your own situation]*	
To prevent accidents and cases of work-related ill health for staff, visitors and contractors, and provide adequate control of health and safety risks arising from work activities			
To provide adequate training to ensure employees are competent to do their work			
To engage and consult with employees on day-to-day health and safety conditions and provide advice and supervision on occupational health			
To implement emergency procedures – evacuation in case of fire or other significant incident. [You can find help with your fire risk assessment at **www.gov.uk/government/organisations/ department-for-communities-and-local-government/series/fire-safety-law-and-guidance-documents-for-business**]			
To maintain safe and healthy working conditions, provide and maintain plant, equipment and machinery, and ensure safe storage/use of substances			
Health and safety law poster is displayed:	*[Location]*		
First-aid box and accident book are located:	*[Location]*		
Accidents and ill health at work reported under RIDDOR (Reporting of Injuries, Diseases and Dangerous Occurrences Regulations 1995) (see www.hse.gov.uk/riddor):			
Signed: (Employer)		**Date:**	
Subject to review, monitoring and revision by:		**Every:** *[12 months or sooner if work activity changes]*	

Published by the Health and Safety Executive 11/11

Annex 1E

Risk assessment

All employers must conduct a risk assessment. Employers with five or more employees have to record the significant findings of their risk assessment.

The risk assessment has been started by including a sample entry for a common hazard to illustrate what is expected (the sample entry is taken from an office-based business). Look at how this might apply to your business, continue by identifying the hazards that are the real priorities in your case and complete the table to suit.

You may find HSE example risk assessments a useful guide (**www.hse.gov.uk/risk/ casestudies/**). Simply choose the example closest to your business.

Practice name:

What are the hazards?	Who might be harmed and how?	What are you already doing?	Do you need to do anything else to manage this risk?	Action by whom?	Action by when?	Done
Slips and trips	Staff and visitors may be injured if they trip over objects or slip on spillages	We carry out general good housekeeping. All areas are well lit including stairs. There are no trailing leads or cables. Staff keep work areas clear, e.g. no boxes left in walkways, deliveries stored immediately, offices cleaned each evening	Better housekeeping is needed in staff kitchen, e.g. on spills	All staff, supervisors to monitor		

- Employers with five or more employees must have a written health and safety policy and risk assessment.
- It is important you discuss your assessment and proposed actions with staff or their representatives.
- You should review your risk assessment if you think it might no longer be valid, e.g. following an accident in the workplace, or if there are any significant changes to the hazards in your workplace, such as new equipment or work activities.

For further information and to view HSE example risk assessments go to **www.hse.gov.uk/risk/casestudies/**

Published by the Health and Safety Executive 11/11

Annex 1F
Central policy, plan and procedure register

Procedure

The policies, plans and procedures listed below will be reviewed by [*name*], using the methodologies indicated. The purpose of the reviews of the policies, plans and procedures will be to:

(a) ascertain the extent and effectiveness of their use throughout the practice;
(b) identify positive and developmental trends and issues arising from their use throughout the practice;
(c) make recommendations for changes that may be needed;
(d) where appropriate, compile a report on the findings of each review to the appropriate body or individual within the practice.

The reviews and any issues arising from them will be documented in the 'Notes from review' column and/or in any other form as required by the practice, including:

• Business and marketing plans, and the services offered by the practice – at least biannually.
• All other policies, plans and procedures – at least annually.

Important requirement

Describe how each policy, plan or procedure will be reviewed in the methodology column (using the initials at the end of each bullet point if desired), e.g.

• data from file reviews (FR);
• data from client satisfaction (CS);
• during management meetings (MM);
• during risk committee/group meetings (RM);
• examination of monitoring documents (MD);
• examination of relevant records maintained by the practice (RR);
• in the light of any regulatory or legislative changes that are relevant to the policy, plan or procedure (L).

Policies

	Person responsible	Date of last review	Review methodology [*Insert brief overview of how the policy will be reviewed*]	Notes from review
Risk management				
Outsourcing				
Equality and diversity				
Health and safety				
Corporate social responsibility (CSR)				
Information management				
Email				
Website management (if practice has a website)				
Internet access (if people have access to the internet)				
Social media (if people have access to social media)				
Training and development				
Performance management				
Conflict of interest				
Client care				

Plans

	Person responsible	Date of last review	Review methodology [*Insert brief overview of how the plan will be reviewed*]	Notes from review
Business plan				
Services that the practice offers				
Marketing plan				
Business continuity plan (BCP)				
IT plan				
Recruitment plan				
Practice wide training plan				

Procedures

	Person responsible	Date of last review	Review methodology [*Insert brief overview of how the procedure will be reviewed*]	Notes from review
Client billing				
Financial transactions				
Prevention of financial crime				
Complaints				
Acceptance and declining of instructions				

2 Strategic plans

2.1 Business plan

2.1 Practices will develop and maintain a business plan which must include:

a: measurable objectives for the next 12 months
b: a recruitment plan
c: the person responsible for the plan
d: a procedure for a review of the plan to be conducted every six months to verify the plan is in effective operation across the practice.

It is important that business plans contain measurable objectives, examples of which could include:

- reduction in administrative costs by x per cent;
- increase in the number of clients, either generally or in specific sectors by x per cent;
- increase in profit margins by x per cent;
- increase in revenue by x per cent.

It is not uncommon for practices to identify measures, but to omit the actual metrics used within the measures.

2.2 Marketing plan

2.2 Practices will develop and maintain a marketing plan which must include:

a: measurable objectives for the next 12 months
b: the person responsible for the plan
c: a procedure for a review of the plan to be conducted every six months to verify the plan is in effective operation across the practice

As with the business plan, the marketing plan must contain measurable objectives together with the metrics that will be used to ascertain the success or otherwise of those objectives. Areas of measurement could include:

- a specified number of marketing initiatives to be undertaken, such as seminars, exhibitions, networking events;
- specified targeting of a particular geographic area or client sector;
- a specified number of new clients, either generally or within a particular sector.

The descriptions of the client groups to be served and how services will be provided often form part of the section of the business plan which describes the background to the practice and the services that it provides. Some practices have a separate service plan. The provision of the services could include activities such as:

- visiting clients at home; and
- late evening or weekend opening.

The recruitment plan can be a separate document. In the current economic climate, many practices are only recruiting when vacancies occur through retirement or people leaving. If this is the case, then it needs to be stated. Many practices often identify likely recruitment needs in individual departmental business plans.

A business plan template is given at **Annex 2A**; a marketing plan template at **Annex 2B**.

2.3 Business continuity planning

2.3 Practices will have a business continuity plan, which must include:

a: an evaluation of potential risks and the likelihood of their impact
b: ways to reduce, avoid and transfer the risks
c: key people relevant to the implementation of the plan
d: the person responsible for the plan
e: a procedure to test the plan annually, to verify that it would be effective in the event of a business interruption.

Business continuity might be something of an alien subject. In many smaller practices, staff may find it difficult to have the time or motivation to pay much attention to it. It was, however, part of the Solicitors' Code of Conduct and having a business continuity plan is now an indicative behaviour for meeting the outcomes relating to management of your business set out in Chapter 7 of the SRA Code of Conduct 2011. It also has other benefits to any business serving the general public or otherwise.

Often, practices tendering for contracts to provide legal services to external organisations, including local authorities and government departments, are required to either produce their business continuity plans, or certify that they meet ISO 22301 (the international standard for business continuity planning).

2.4 Resources

The business continuity plan will need to be appropriate for your practice. The pressures on a small practice are going to be very different from those with large multi-site operations. There is no point in a business continuity plan that uses so much of your practice's resources (time and money) that it impacts in a negative way on your day-to-day work. Often practices will find out that they are already providing for business continuity and it is just a case of setting out the procedures in the plan then taking them a stage further to ensure that risks are dealt with proportionately and appropriately.

If you seek more detailed guidance on business continuity planning, including a planning template, see the *Lexcel Business Continuity Planning Toolkit* (Law Society, 2011).

Below are some of the risks that all practices may want to consider.

2.4.1 Fire

- Who is responsible for the fire management processes/policies?
- What problems would arise if there was a fire while people were in the building?
- What is the frequency and effectiveness of any fire drills and evacuation plans?
- What would happen if there was a fire while the office was closed?
- How would the practice restart business?
- How would the practice communicate with staff and clients?
- Does the practice have alternative premises to use in the event of a fire damaging the office?

2.4.2 Flood

- How likely is the risk of a flood?
- What would the practice do about IT systems in the event of a flood?
- What would the practice do about recovery of hard copy documents?
- Does the threat of flood affect where any information assets are stored?

2.4.3 IT

- What back-ups of IT data does the practice undertake?
- Where are back-ups stored? Are they taken off site to a secure location?
- What would happen in the event of a power interruption? Would the computers safely shut down without destroying any data?
- If the power interruption were more than a temporary disruption, what would the practice do?

2.4.4 Personnel

- What would happen if a key member of staff were incapacitated for a period of time, for example, on long-term sick leave? Is there anyone with sufficient knowledge to be able to fill in for them?
- What would the practice do in the event of an influenza pandemic? What plans does the practice have in place in case an influenza pandemic occurs, both to protect those at work and to cover for those who are off work?

2.4.5 Communication

- How would the practice communicate with staff and clients in the event of a communications breakdown, for example, a sustained loss of the practice's telephone system?
- How would the practice communicate with staff and clients in the event of a closure of the main office because of fire or some other eventuality?
- How would the practice deal with a key member of staff getting into trouble or being arrested to prevent reputational damage (which could do as much damage as any physical disaster)?

2.5 What to do with a business continuity plan

A business continuity plan that, once finished, is locked away and forgotten about is a waste of all the resources invested in it. It is important that all staff are aware of it and the relevant parts are communicated to those staff who need to know. The plan will need to be reviewed at least annually and updated, with any changes being communicated to everyone.

2.5.1 Testing the plan

The Lexcel standard requires that there is a procedure for testing the plan at least annually to verify that it is effective in operation across the practice.

Ways of testing the plan can include:

- fire drills, which should be a regular feature of testing the plan;
- implementing the telephone cascade system;
- testing the IT back-up to ensure it is effective and shuts down safely;
- switching to alternative banking facilities;
- testing alternative communication systems.

2.6 The IT plan

The size of the IT plan often depends on the size of the practice and its use of IT. In addition to describing the IT facilities within the practice and the way in which they are used to provide services to clients, the plan must contain a description of the actual or anticipated IT developments for the forthcoming year. These developments could be as simple as the replacement of printers, photocopiers and PCs, and the updating of software.

Regardless of how large or small the intended development of IT, it needs to be documented.

2.7 People plan

A practice's greatest asset, and greatest risk, can be its staff. Managing the structure, quantity and performance of your people can have a significant impact on the success of the practice.

Engaging and communicating with staff can lead to increased commitment and performance. Practices should consider conducting staff surveys as a regular form of gaining feedback on set activities, as well as ad hoc projects or tasks.

For a template people plan, see **Annex 2C**. For a list of key performance indicators (KPIs) relevant to people planning, see **Annex 2D**.

Annex 2A
Business plan template

[*Year*] business plan

Author: [*name of person responsible for producing plan*]

Approver: [*name of person responsible for final review and sign-off*]

Reviewer: [*name of any colleagues responsible for reviewing plan*]

Contributors: [*names of any colleagues contributing to production of plan*]

Date: [*date*]

Version: v[*number*]

Contents

1   Objectives
2   Key performance indicators (KPIs)
3   Budget
4   Resources
5   Products and services
6   Clients and market
7   Business development and marketing
8   Operational infrastructure
9   Risks
10 Policy statements
11 Recommendations
Annex A: [*name of practice/unit/department/team*] budget
Annex B: [*name of practice/unit/department/team*] structure

1   Objectives

The high level objectives for [*name of practice/unit/department/team*] for [*year*] are:

[*Outline of objectives here*]

2   Key performance indicators (KPIs)

KPI	Target	Owner

3   Budget

Expenditure is budgeted at £[*value*]. Income has been targeted at £[*value*]. Please see Annex A for the [*year*] budget for [*name of practice/unit/department/team*].

4   Resources

Overview

[*Name of practice/unit/department/team*] currently employs [*number*] permanent and [*number*] temporary staff. We currently have [*number*] [teams/departments/ practice areas] within our remit. An outline of our [practice/unit/department/team] structure and breakdown of staff can be found in Annex B.

Factors affecting resources

[*Outline factors*]

5   Products and services

[*Product/service 1*]

[*Outline of product/service*]

[*Product/service 2*]

[*Outline of product/service*]

[*Product/service 3*]

[*Outline of product/service*]

6   Clients and market

Client segmentation

[*Outline, including graphical representations where possible*]

Market forces and adoption

[*Outline, including graphical representations where possible*]

7   Business development and marketing

Budget

The business development/marketing budget for [*name of practice/unit/department/ team*] for [*year*] is £[*value*].

Targets

Our key marketing audiences for [*year*] are:

- [*Audience*]

Overall management

[*Outline*]

Team and individual responsibilities

[*Outline*]

Lead generation

[*Outline*]

Campaign focuses

- Topics – [*outline*]
- Audience segments – [*outline*]
- Geographic targets – [*outline*]
- Product/service launches – [*outline*]

Activities

Promotional activities for [*name of practice/unit/department/team*] in [*year*] will include:

- Materials – [*outline*]
- Events – [*outline*]
- Publications – [*outline*]
- PR – [*outline*]
- Direct mail – [*outline*]
- Advertising – [*outline*]
- Cross-marketing – [*outline*]

- [Practice/department] website(s) – [*outline*]
- External website(s) – [*outline*]

8 Operational infrastructure

Human resources

[Outline, including graphical representations where possible]

Finance

[Outline, including graphical representations where possible]

IT

[Outline, including graphical representations where possible]

Facilities

[Outline, including graphical representations where possible]

9 Risks

Regulatory

[Outline]

Strategic

[Outline]

Operational

[Outline]

Financial

[Outline]

Competition/reputational

[Outline]

Technological

[Outline]

10 Policy statements

Equality and diversity statement

[Practice's equality and diversity statement]

Corporate and social responsibility statement

[Practice's corporate and social responsibility statement]

11 Recommendations

[Recommendation heading]

[Outline]

Annex A: [*name of practice/unit/department/team*] budget

[Year] budget
Cost centre: [*reference*]
Project reference: [*reference*]

	J	F	M	A	M	J	J	A	S	O	N	D	Year budget	Year actual	Variance
Income															
[*Item code*] Fees													£0	£0	£0
[*Item code*] Interest													£0	£0	£0
[*Item code*] Course and function income													£0	£0	£0
[*Item code*] Commission/licence income													£0	£0	£0
[*Item code*] Sponsorship income													£0	£0	£0
[*Item code*] Sundry income													£0	£0	£0
Total income	£0	£0	£0	£0	£0	£0	£0	£0	£0	£0	£0	£0	£0	£0	£0
Staff expenditure															
[*Item code*] Basic salaries													£0	£0	£0
[*Item code*] NIC													£0	£0	£0
[*Item code*] Agency staff													£0	£0	£0
[*Item code*] Medical insurance													£0	£0	£0
[*Item code*] Employee benefit costs													£0	£0	£0
Non-staff expenditure															
[*Item code*] Stationery supplies													£0	£0	£0
[*Item code*] External printing and duplicating services													£0	£0	£0
[*Item code*] Telecommunication costs													£0	£0	£0

[Year] budget

Cost centre: *[reference]*

Project reference: *[reference]*

		J	F	M	A	M	J	J	A	S	O	N	D	Year budget	Year actual	Variance
[Item code]	Document exchange payment													£0	£0	£0
[Item code]	Postage													£0	£0	£0
[Item code]	Courier service													£0	£0	£0
[Item code]	Internal meetings													£0	£0	£0
[Item code]	Staff accommodation/ meals and subsistence													£0	£0	£0
[Item code]	Taxis and car hire													£0	£0	£0
[Item code]	Non-employee expenses													£0	£0	£0
[Item code]	Conferences, exhibitions and room hire													£0	£0	£0
[Item code]	Consultancy and services													£0	£0	£0
[Item code]	Conference fees													£0	£0	£0
[Item code]	Business development/ marketing													£0	£0	£0
[Item code]	Sundry expenses													£0	£0	£0
[Item code]	Books													£0	£0	£0
[Item code]	Audio visual materials/ equipment													£0	£0	£0
[Item code]	Doubtful debts provision movement													£0	£0	£0
Total expenditure		£0	£0	£0	£0	£0	£0	£0	£0	£0	£0	£0	£0	£0	£0	£0
Total net position		£0	£0	£0	£0	£0	£0	£0	£0	£0	£0	£0	£0	£0	£0	£0

Annex B: [*name of practice/unit/department/team*] structure

[Insert organisation chart(s) or tables – example below]

Job title	[*Unit/department/team*]	Quantity	Main role responsibilities

Annex 2B
Marketing plan template

Marketing plan [*year*]

Contents

1   Introduction
2   Branding
3   Target audiences
4   Audience segmentation
5   Market propositions
6   Activities
7   Key milestones
8   Recommendations

1   Introduction

[*Outline of marketing plan*]

2   Branding

Market awareness

[*Overview*]

Existing users

[*Overview of those using visual identity*]

3   Target audiences

[*Overview of target audiences for marketing campaigns*]

4   Audience segmentation

[*Overview of target audience segments*]

Decision makers

Definition: [*outline of person with decision-making authority in target organisation*]

Group	Target	Decision maker	Influencers	Benefit

Influencers

Definition: [*outline of person/people who can influence the decision maker*]

Group	Target	Decision maker	Influencers	Benefit

Early adopters

Definition: [*outline of person/people who is/are likely to adopt product or service more quickly than others in target organisation*]

Group	Target	Decision maker	Influencers	Benefit

5   Market propositions

Tier 1

[*Details of highest level propositions*]

Tier 2

[Details of second highest level propositions]

6   Activities

Events

Title	Audience figure target	Focus	Budget	Occurrence

Direct mail

Title	Audience figure target	Focus	Budget	Occurrence

Public relations

Publication	Audience figure target	Message	Budget	Occurrence

Advertising

Publication	Audience figure target	Message	Budget	Occurrence

Website

[*Outline*]

7   Key milestones

Title	Description	Owner	Timescale

8   Recommendations

[*Recommendation title*]

[*Outline*]

Annex 2C

People plan

The person with overall responsibility for the people plan is [*name*].

The practice is committed to delivering a quality service to all clients by ensuring that we have the right number of people in the relevant locations with the appropriate skills and knowledge to deliver an efficient and effective service.

Our people planning process takes place on [*date*] during the strategic planning cycle. A review of our people plan is conducted every time there in a change in staff levels as a result of consistently increased work levels.

Job role	Current numbers	Proposed numbers for next financial year	Increases/ decreases	Year 2 increases/ decreases	Year 3 increases/ decreases
Partners/directors/head of legal					
Associates					
Solicitors					
Trainee solicitors					
Legal executives					
Other fee earners					
Administrators					
Secretaries					
Others					
Totals					
Fee income					
% staff costs to fee income					

Annex 2D

People planning: key performance indicators (KPIs)

KPIs are measures of performance at [*name of practice*]. They will reflect the factors that are essential to, and will drive and underpin, the achievement of your objectives. For example, (a) management development and change, and (b) employees noticing the change and increasing productivity, may be drivers to the outcome of (c) increased sales.

Strategic objective	Key performance indicators	Action	Outcome
To ensure that our business objectives are met by having sufficient manpower available at all times.	• Ensure that the right numbers of people are available at the right time with the appropriate skills and knowledge we require. • Where possible encourage job enrichment and improve job satisfaction. • Monitor people needs and evaluate replacement methods where possible.	To determine the people needs by department/team at least annually.	• Current levels of staff identified by using staff cost to income generation formula to identify needs and risks to the practice and profitability. • Identify how many staff are employed by job category now and how many are needed by department/team. • Identify how many staff are retiring and where the replacements are coming from. • Consider whether de-skilling job roles is a solution. Can trainees be used with closer supervision?
		Evaluate people needs.	• Can new equipment or technology negate the need? • Are there other solutions, e.g. job enrichment, job rotation, job enlargement? • Will a productivity bonus negate the need? • Will additional training and development reduce the need?

Strategic objective	Key performance indicators	Action	Outcome
		Evaluate external labour market and impact on retention of your own staff.	• What are local unemployment statistics and are the skills and knowledge you require readily available? • What is the local competition that may attract your staff?

3 Financial management

Managing financial performance is critical to the success of your practice. Robust budgeting will provide assurances not only to the management of a practice, but its staff and key stakeholders such as insurers and lenders.

Monitoring income and expenditure should be undertaken on a frequent basis to ensure you are aware of the stability and impacting factors to your business. Re-forecasting will help track any potential changes in income or expenditure, enabling the practice to manage any changes these may result in.

Only one person should be identified with this responsibility. Wherever the person responsible for financial management resides or whatever their job title, they must have all the relevant qualifications, experience, skills and authority to effectively manage your practice's finances.

3.1 Responsibility for financial management

3.1 Practices will document responsibility for overall financial management.

As part of a practice's management arrangements, it is important that it is clear who is responsible for financial management. For most practices, the responsibility will lie with the compliance officer for finance and administration (COFA) and this should be reflected in the office manual.

The following statement may be used:

[*Name*] has direct responsibility for overseeing and managing financial affairs. [S/he] is also the practice's compliance officer for finance and administration (COFA).

3.2 Documentary evidence

3.2 Practices will be able to provide documentary evidence of their financial management procedure, including:

   a: annual budget including, income and expenditure
   b: annual income and expenditure accounts
   c: annual balance sheet
   d: annual income and expenditure forecast to be reviewed quarterly
   e: variance analysis conducted at least quarterly of income and expenditure against budgets
   f: quarterly variance analysis which includes at least their cash flow

To meet the requirements of 3.2 of the Lexcel standard, practices need to demonstrate that they comply with six specific areas of financial management. Practices may decline to share financial data with their assessor and in such cases the assessor will require copies of correspondence from the practice's accountant confirming the above requirements have been adhered to.

3.3 Time recording procedure

3.3 Practices will have a time recording procedure which enables:

    a: the accurate measurement of time spent on matters for billing purposes
    b: the monitoring of work in progress

The monitoring of time is mandatory where time is a factor for billing, but can also be a useful management tool. Practices should also consider how abortive fixed fee work will be charged to clients. If it is to be based on time spent, then there would be a need to time record in such matters.

Monitoring work in progress (WIP) helps practices in reviewing the status of a matter as well as the performance of staff. It can enable risks to be identified earlier and thus implement solutions to mitigate any risk and associated impact. Monitoring WIP also helps to keep clients informed of fee earning hours and associated costs.

3.4 Procedure for billing clients

3.4 Practices will have a procedure in relation to billing clients, including:

    a: the frequency and terms for billing clients
    b: credit limits for new and existing clients
    c: procedure to manage debts
    d: the person responsible for the procedures
    e: a documented review of the procedures at least annually, to verify they are in effective operation across the practice.

The procedure in relation to billing clients needs to indicate whether the practice extends credit limits to clients. If it does not have any specific credit limits, then the procedure needs to make that point. The procedure needs to make it clear how often fee earners are required to bill clients. This is likely to vary, depending on the nature of matters.

The procedure for managing debts is often referred to as 'credit control'.

Some practices may consider having one set of procedures that deal with billing and financial transactions.

3.5 Financial transactions procedure

3.5 Practices will have a procedure for the handling of financial transactions including:

a: the person responsible for the procedures
b: a documented review of the procedures at least annually, to verify they are in effective operation across the practice.

It is quite likely that practices already have procedures to deal with financial transactions, which include such activities and issues as (this list is not exhaustive):

* authorised signatories;
* accounts enquiries;
* file closing/archiving;
* disbursements;
* cheque requests;
* petty cash;
* motor and travel expenses;
* cancelled cheque requests;
* un-presented/expired cheques;
* banking/remittance received;
* client to office/office to client transfers;
* billing (and time posting);
* write-off requests;
* procedure for billing clients;
* credit control;
* prompt return of client monies.

4 Information management

4.1 Information management policy

4.1 Practices will have an information management policy, which must include:

    a: the identification of relevant information assets of both the practice and clients
    b: the risk to these assets, their likelihood and their impact
    c: procedures for the protection and security of the information assets
    d: a procedure for training personnel
    e: the person responsible for the policy
    f: a procedure for an annual review of the policy, to verify it is in effective operation across the practice.

The Lexcel standard requires practices to address the issue of information management and to support and promote this through a written information management policy and supporting processes and procedures.

What difference will your information management policy make in practice? You will be more organised, clearer about what you are doing and better able to manage valuable information assets. You will also be able to identify and mitigate risks and control costs.

For an information management policy, see **Annex 4A**.

4.2 Email policy

4.2 Practices will have an e-mail policy, which must include:

    a: the scope of permitted and prohibited use
    b: procedures for monitoring personnel using e-mail
    c: procedures for the management and security of e-mails
    d: procedures for the storage and destruction of e-mails
    e: the person responsible for the policy
    f: a procedure for an annual review of the policy, to verify it is in effective operation across the practice.

Technological innovations in personal and group communications have spread rapidly and they are likely to continue to do so. As devices and applications increasingly have multiple uses, old boundaries are dissolving. This is especially true in relation to the internet, email, social networking sites, blogs, Twitter, instant messaging and smartphones. This means that your email along with your website management and internet access policies could form part of a wider personal communications policy. They will certainly need to sit comfortably alongside it or contain other relevant policies and should also reflect the broad principles established by your information management policy.

You should consider your email policy at two basic levels:

1. **The system level** – covering the identification, selection, deployment and periodic review of email systems by the practice.
2. **The individual level** – covering the training, supporting and guiding of groups and individuals in using these systems for business and personal activity.

For a policy on email, see **Annex 4B**.

4.3 Website policy

4.3 If the practice has a website, the practice must have a website management policy, which must include:

    a: a procedure for content approval, publishing and removal
    b: the scope of permitted and prohibited content
    c: procedures for the management of its security
    d: the person responsible for the policy
    e: a procedure for an annual review of the policy, to verify it is in effective operation across the practice.

The key to an effective website is thinking about its purpose from the users' point of view. This may appear obvious but can still be quite difficult to achieve. Consider the following:

*   You need to identify and understand your users.
*   You need to be able to translate user needs into an effective site.
*   You should avoid making your initial question 'What do we want our site to say about us?' Clearly your site will say many things about you – that you do not understand the online needs of your clients or potential clients should not be one of them.
*   Your users and their needs will change over time.

You should consider your website management policy at two basic levels:

1. **The system level** – covering the identification, selection, deployment and review of your website infrastructure.
2. **The individual level** – covering the support and guidance of groups and individuals in maintaining, updating and interacting with your website.

For a policy on website management, see **Annex 4C**.

4.4 Internet access

4.4 If personnel in the practice have Internet access the practice must have an Internet access policy, which must include:

    a: the scope of permitted and prohibited use
    b: procedures for monitoring personnel accessing the Internet
    c: the person responsible for the policy
    d: a procedure for an annual review of the policy, to verify it is in effective operation across the practice.

For a policy on internet access, see **Annex 4D**.

4.5 Social media

With the increasing use of social media, a requirement to have a social media policy has been added to Lexcel v5. Social media has many definitions but is essentially any online media platform that provides content for users and allows users to participate in the creation or development of that content. Some examples of online media platforms include:

- forums and comment spaces, e.g. RollOnFriday, BBC and the Guardian;
- social networking websites, e.g. Facebook and LinkedIn;
- microblogging sites, e.g. Twitter.

Practices must carefully consider their participation in social media as it can be a significant reputational, strategic and operational risk. The Law Society has published a practice note on social media which gives guidance on how to set up a social media policy and areas to look out for.

The practice note can be found at: **www.lawsociety.org.uk/productsandservices/practicenotes/socialmedia/5049.article**

Practices may wish to produce guidelines for staff who wish to participate in social media channels in which they are identifiable as employees of the practice. Factors to consider are:

- lists of approved websites;
- use of practice logos and other branding guidelines;
- policies and procedures for making reference to the practice, any associated products, services when participating in social media in a personal capacity;
- approval procedure for adding content.

Alternatively, practices may choose to prohibit staff from engaging in any type of social media where they represent the practice. If this is the case, practices need to make this clear to staff and any consequences if staff fail to adhere to this.

For a policy on social media, see **Annex 4E**.

Annex 4A
Information management policy

Policy statement

The practice recognises the importance of ensuring the safety and security of the information that it holds in electronic and hard/documentary form. This policy contains details of the practice's approach to the subject of information management, and contains procedures and principles that are to be followed by everyone in the practice.

Any breaches of this policy could have far reaching and serious consequences for the practice, and it is essential that it is complied with at all times. Breaches of the policy will be treated as extremely serious by the practice, and could result in disciplinary proceedings.

Scope

This policy covers information created, and assets held, by the practice.

This policy applies to all individuals working at every level and grade, including partners, senior managers, officers, directors, employees, consultants, contractors, trainees, home workers, part-time and fixed-term employees, casual and agency staff and volunteers, collectively referred to as staff in this policy.

Third parties who have access to the practice's electronic communication systems and equipment are also required to comply with this policy.

Purpose

The policy is intended to eliminate mismanagement of data wherever possible, in order to avoid or mitigate some or all of the following consequences (the list is not exhaustive):

- proceedings under the Data Protection Act 1998;
- the inability to offer services;
- reputational and/or financial damage;
- proceedings for negligence;
- breaches of confidentiality;
- breaches of the SRA Code of Conduct 2011 and any other legislative or regulatory requirements.

Categories of information assets

The practice holds electronic and hard copy (mainly paper) information assets, as detailed below (the list is not exhaustive).

1. *Hard/document-based information assets*

- Practice documents (leases, standard forms, minutes, etc.).
- Client documents (letters, agreements, court orders, bill of costs, etc.).
- HR staff documents (contracts, holiday and sickness records, etc.).
- Precedents (departmental paragraphs, etc.).
- Marketing customer relationship management (CRM) (contact information, event acceptance, etc.).
- Templates and forms (departmental).
- Financial (practice reports, analysis spreadsheets, etc.).

2. *Electronic information assets*

The electronic information assets are described in the table below, together with descriptions of how they, and 'hard' information assets, are retained and stored by the practice.

[*Each practice will need to make amendments that represent their assets and individual approaches and responsibilities for those assets within the table. The information presently in the table is an example of one practice's approach.*]

Asset description	Media type	Format type	Backup type	Lead responsibility
'Hard' assets as described above	Paper	Within cabinet drawers and paper folders/lever arch folders	Archiving house and business continuity planning	Fee earners and practice manager

Identified risks associated with the data held

The following table outlines the potential risks associated with the data assets identified above, together with measures that the practice takes to prevent, minimise or mitigate those risks. References to BCP mean the business continuity plan, and DRP mean the disaster recovery plan.

Risk description	First line	Second line
Fire/flood/major incident	• Key documents retained in metal cabinets and fireproof safe/cupboard • 'Hard' assets retained in cabinets and shelves above floor level • Key documents scanned for electronic storage	Annual risk assessment with operational BCP and DRP
Virus attacks	Practice wide antivirus software. Training and awareness training on regulations, operational procedures and policies	Full backups of data on internal and external data storage solutions
Damaging integrity of data through lack of knowledge or malice	Training and awareness training on regulations, operational procedures and policies	Full backups of data on internal and external data storage solutions
Password sharing	Training and awareness training on regulations, operational procedures and policies	Reinforcement of security requirements at team meetings
Remote connection	Full SSL (Secure Sockets Layer) VPN connections for all external connecting devices (including laptops, PDAs)	
External attack	Full firewall protection	Full backups of data on internal and external data storage solutions

Management roles and responsibilities

Responsibility for the management of electronic data lies with [name], and the responsibility for hard information assets lies with:

- fee earners in the case of such assets relevant to the matter files; and
- [name] for all other such assets.

The responsibilities include (the list is not exhaustive):

- management and security of the data;
- ensuring that the data conforms to all policies relating to its use, retention and storage;

- ensuring that company records are created, maintained and archived in accordance with the relevant policies;
- management of all records;
- management of risks to the data;
- ensuring that sufficient resources are devoted to these tasks.

Training

Training on information management forms part of the induction process for new partners, fee earners and members of staff. Additionally, it is included in the list of 'generic' training that applies to all members of the practice, and which will be delivered as indicated in the practice's training plan at intervals not exceeding [*frequency with which this training will be provided*].

At the discretion of managers and team leaders, training can also be presented at ad hoc intervals during team/departmental meetings.

Information management principles and guidance

The practice's management and use of information assets will comply with the seven information management principles given below.

1. Information is a corporate resource which belongs to the practice and its clients.

As a consequence, information must be:

Available

2. Staff will only limit colleagues' access to information that they create or capture if its sensitivity requires it.
3. Information will be managed consistently, including by the use of approved naming conventions and filing structures.

Appropriate

4. Everyone will ensure that information is accurate and fit for purpose.
5. Information will be retained and disposed of appropriately.
6. Everyone is personally responsible for the effective management of the information that they create, capture or use.
7. In managing information, everyone will comply with the relevant statutory and regulatory requirements – including the requirement not to destroy information where there is a legal obligation to retain it.

Information security

A common sense approach must be taken to information security. Individuals are responsible for the security of information that they create or store. Particular care should be exercised with information that may be commercially sensitive (e.g.

relating to project plans or bid tenders). When dealing with paper documents, this includes locking filing cabinets and, when dealing with electronic data, the facility to change folder and file user access rights.

Storage and retrieval of information

A consistent approach is important to preserve the quality and integrity of information, and to ensure that it can be readily identified and retrieved.

Staff should consider the retrieval needs of others within the practice when storing information. For example, this could require the use of document titles, and the addition of relevant keywords in order to enable others to retrieve the document. This is particularly important with regard to emails.

Documents should be placed within the practice's network storage facilities at the earliest opportunity, in order to help prevent information from becoming outdated before others, who may have an interest in it, can gain access.

Dissemination of information

Anyone who receives information which is not relevant to them must pass it to an appropriate individual within the practice who can determine whether it should be retained.

There will be times when consideration should be given as to whether information should be published on the practice's intranet, and this may mean seeking advice from [name].

Retention and disposal of information

Information that is inaccurate or out of date should not be kept (unless it has a historical value). Indeed, keeping inaccurate information can be damaging. Information that is no longer required for business purposes, or in order to comply with a legal obligation, should be deleted or destroyed.

Certain information, including matter files, is retained as indicated in [location of where file retention periods are indicated].

Intellectual property of others (copyright)

A document will not incorporate the intellectual property of others unless the practice has the relevant rights. Documents (including scanning) must not be entered into the information system unless the practice owns or has obtained the copyright to do so. Material specifically addressed to the practice can be entered into the information management system.

Data Protection Act 1998

Everyone is responsible for complying with the eight principles relating to personal information (summarised below) that are contained in the Data Protection Act 1998.

Such information must:

1. be fairly and lawfully processed;
2. be processed for specified purposes;
3. be adequate, relevant and not excessive;
4. be accurate and, where necessary, kept up to date;
5. not be kept for longer than is necessary;
6. be processed in line with the rights of the individual;
7. be kept secure; and
8. not be transferred to countries outside the European Economic Area unless the information is adequately protected.

Policy review

[*Name*] will conduct a documented review of this policy at least annually to ensure that it is current, and in effective use throughout the practice.

Relevant definitions

Document

A 'document' can be defined as information that is stored as a single entity on some medium, e.g. on a computer drive or paper file, etc.

The term also covers information in what might seem non-documentary formats, e.g. computer applications and databases.

Record

A 'record' can be defined as a document which has content, context and structure, and which provides evidence of a business transaction, or contains information needed to carry on the practice's business.

A record can either be created within or without the practice. It may be created to fulfil a legal requirement, and may be required as evidence or to satisfy accountability.

Records are derived from documents, therefore all records will be documents, but not all documents will be records. For example, a publication in a library provides information, and is therefore a document, but it is not a record because it does not provide evidence of an activity.

Annex 4B
Email policy

1   Person with overall responsibility

1.1 The person with overall responsibility for the email policy is [*name and job title*]. Technical questions, including security matters, should be addressed to [*name or function/job title and contact details*].

2   General approach to the use of email

2.1 [*Name of practice*] provides the following systems for business use: [*briefly outline the email and related facilities offered by the practice, e.g.*

- *standard email facilities (e.g. Microsoft Outlook)*
- *webmail facilities*
- *push email facilities (e.g. RIM's BlackBerry)*
- *encryption services*
- *remote access to emails*
- *facilities for sending personal emails*]

2.2 Email facilities should only be used where you have [*the explicit authority of your line manager/written authority*] to do so. Your use of a system must be in accordance with the conditions or restrictions brought to your attention at the time of authorisation and as amended from time to time, which can be found at [location of any conditions or restrictions].

2.3 Staff who have been granted access to email facilities are responsible for ensuring that:

- they only use appropriate templates/system-produced drafts, or, where these are not available, that they follow the practice's style and content protocol which can be found at [*location of more detailed guidance*]; and
- they follow the [practice's/department's] review and approval procedure by [*referring drafts to their line manager/following the workflow process*].

2.4 If staff are uncertain about the correct procedure to follow they should always consult their line manager. They should never rely on their own authority.

3   Permitted and prohibited use of email

Personal use of email

3.1 Staff are not permitted to use the practice's email facilities for non-business purposes.

3.2 In exceptional circumstances, you may apply to your line manager for permission to send a non-business related email. Your manager will consider this request and may make special arrangements to allow you to send such an email [using a dedicated machine].

3.3 [*Name of practice*] discourages the receipt of non-business related emails and you should make this clear to potential correspondents.

Avoid defamatory, offensive and obscene emails

3.4 You should never send emails that could be construed as defamatory. Further information is located at [*location of guidance and/or a training course*]. If in doubt do not send; consult your line manager.

3.5 You should never compose or distribute emails that could be construed as offensive or obscene. Examples of the sort of material that [name of practice] would consider offensive or obscene include:

- [*Examples*]

> **Note:** The Information Commissioner's Employment Practices Data Protection Code suggests that '[a] simple ban on "offensive material" is unlikely to be sufficiently clear for people to know what is and is not allowed' and recommends providing examples.

Avoid inadvertent contracts by email

3.6 It is possible to form a contract by email. You should take care not to do so. Further information on this topic is available at [*location of guidance and/or a training course*].

Avoid distributing copyright material

3.7 You should avoid downloading copyright material from the internet (or obtaining it from other sources) and should not distribute copyright material by email. Further information is available at [*location of guidance and/or a training course*].

4   Email monitoring

4.1 The practice monitors all incoming and outgoing emails. This monitoring is conducted for the purpose of [*explain the purpose of the monitoring*]. The monitoring covers [*explain the extent of the monitoring*] and it is carried out by means of [*explain how the monitoring is carried out*].

5   Email management and security

5.1 You are responsible for the security of the emails you send. Resources for guidance, training and support in information security, including email security, are available to all staff at [*location of guidance, etc.*]. Please contact [*name/role and contact details*] for help and advice. To report a security incident please contact [*name/role and contact details*] or in emergencies or outside business hours contact [*name/role and contact details*].

6   Annual review

6.1 This policy will be reviewed annually on [*date*] by [*name of relevant member in senior management team*] as part of the annual review of the information management system.

6.2 If you have any suggestions for how this policy could be improved please contact [*name and contact details of relevant member in senior management team or delegate*].

Annex 4C
Website management policy

1   Person with overall responsibility

1.1 The person with overall responsibility for the [*name of practice*] website(s) is [*name and job title*].

1.2 [His/her] responsibilities include [*list of responsibilities and decision-making powers. You may also wish to exclude certain powers, for example, budget authorisation above a certain level. If so, how these decisions will be taken could be included in the policy*].

2   Our website

[*Set out the business objectives and plans for your website. A simple statement of the practice's objectives in relation to the site, how it will achieve them and how it plans to develop the site will help to clarify these matters and ensure that they are communicated throughout the practice. This section could include a general statement about the practice's approach to management of the site – a tight, centrally controlled approach or one which allows content owners more autonomy.*]

3   Website management

3.1 Day-to-day operational control questions, including security matters, should be addressed to [*name or function/job title and contact details*].

3.2 Other roles include [*list roles. If you have a large site with many different roles and responsibilities you may wish to set these out in a table along with contact details. Alternatively you may wish to simply put the principal contact in your policy and set out other roles and responsibilities in a separate document. This section should be distinguished from section 4 where key roles in relation to document approval and publishing should be identified.*]

4   Document approval and publishing

4.1 Final responsibility for approving new or revised documents for publication on the website rests with [*name(s) and role(s)*].

4.2 In this context 'document' includes [*list of types of publication that are subject to the approval and publication process*] and excludes [*for example, blogs, etc.*].

4.3 Before publication is approved they [*or you if this is delegated to content owners*] will need to be satisfied that the document meets the required standards in the following areas:

4.3.1 Compliance: [*set out standards of compliance and person responsible for sign-off*]

4.3.2 Quality: [*set out standards of quality and person responsible for sign-off*]

4.3.3 Conformance: [*set out standards of conformance and person responsible for sign-off*]

4.4 They will also need to be satisfied that a review period or expiry date has been set.

5   Permitted and prohibited use

[*This section is most appropriate for setting out the limits of any delegated authority to update the content of the site, rather than regulatory compliance. How you intend to comply with, for example, the Electronic Commerce Directive can either be dealt with in section 4.3 above – by identifying the person required to sign-off a document – or in a separate document. The latter option is probably best.*]

6   Security and content management

6.1 Website security forms part of our overall information security policy which can be found at [*location of policy*].

6.2 Resources for guidance, training and support in information security, including website security, are available to all staff at [*location of guidance, etc.*]. Please contact [*name/role and contact details*] for help and advice. To report a security incident please contact [*name/role and contact details*] or in an emergency or after business hours contact [*name/role and contact details*].

7   Annual review

7.1 This policy will be reviewed annually on [*date*] by [*name of relevant member in senior management team*] as part of the annual review of the information management system.

7.2 If you have any suggestions for how this policy could be improved please contact [*name and contact details of relevant member in senior management team or delegate*].

Annex 4D
Internet access policy

1   Person with overall responsibility

The person with overall responsibility for the internet access policy is [*name and job title*]. Technical questions, including requests to access blocked sites and any security issues, should be addressed to [*name or function/job title and contact details*].

2   General approach to using the internet

[**2.1** [*Name of practice*] provides you with internet access in order to enable you to access information, news and social networking sites that will assist you in carrying out your work, keeping you informed and promoting the practice. [If you intend to publish on a social networking site and can be identified as an employee of [*name of practice*] you should consult our guidelines which can be found at [*location*].]]

[*OR*]

[**2.1** Internet facilities should only be used where you have [*the explicit authority of your line manager/written authority*] to do so. Your use of any internet facilities must be in accordance with the conditions or restrictions brought to your attention at the time of authorisation and as amended from time to time which can be found at [*location of any conditions or restrictions*].]

3   Permitted and prohibited use of the internet

3.1 You are permitted to make reasonable personal use of the internet during working hours. Staff are expected to use their discretion in doing so.

3.2 You should not access websites that could be deemed offensive or obscene. If you inadvertently access such a site you should leave it. Failure to do so could result in disciplinary action as set out in [*location of relevant staff handbook*]. Examples of material deemed offensive by [*name of practice*] are:

*   [*Examples*]

> **Note:** The Information Commissioner's Employment Practices Data Protection Code suggests that: 'In the case of internet access, specify clearly any restrictions on material that can be viewed or copied. A simple ban on "offensive material" is unlikely to be sufficiently clear for people to know what is and is not allowed.' It suggests providing examples of the sort of material that is considered offensive, such as material containing racist terminology or nudity.

3.3 You should take care not to download material or access internet services that could pose a threat to the security of [*name of practice's*] systems. All staff should have received training in [*title of training course*] and if you are in doubt you should consult [*name, job title and contact details*].

3.4 You should not enter into a contract or purchase goods and services on behalf of [*name of practice*] on the internet. Further information on this topic is available at [*location of guidance and/or a training course*].

3.5 You should avoid downloading copyright material from the internet unless you are entitled to do so. Further information can be found at [*location of guidance and/or a training course*].

4   Monitoring of internet use

4.1 [*Name of practice*] monitors staff internet use and keeps a record of each website you visit and the duration of your visit. This monitoring is conducted for the purpose of [*explain the purpose of the monitoring*]. The monitoring covers [*explain the extent of the monitoring*] and it is carried out by means of [*explain how the monitoring is carried out*].

5   Internet management and security

5.1 [*Name of practice*] uses tools to automatically block access to certain websites and to automatically monitor its systems to prevent security breaches. If you need to access a website that has been blocked you should contact [*name, job title and contact details*]. You may be asked to explain why you need access to the blocked website.

6   Annual review

6.1 This policy will be reviewed annually on [*date*] by [*name of relevant member in senior management team*] as part of the annual review of the information management system.

6.2 If you have any suggestions for how this policy could be improved please contact [*name and contact details of relevant member in senior management team or delegate*].

Annex 4E

Social media policy

[Statement or policy example where social media is not in use]

[If your practice does not participate in social media, you should issue a statement to highlight this policy to all staff to ensure they are aware and understand their obligations. This will help mitigate the risk of social media being participated in for or on behalf of the practice incorrectly.]

[Name of practice] does not participate in or use social media sites e.g. Facebook, Twitter [insert further examples as required]. [Name] is responsible for reviewing the practice's participation in and use of social media in our practice. [He/she] must be informed of any breaches and will conduct a review of participation or use at least annually.

[Name of practice] recognises that employees may wish to participate in or use social media for personal use. No employee must in any way bring the practice, its staff, its existing or prospective clients or third party individuals/entities connected to the practice into disrepute or publish any information, particularly anything confidential or sensitive, relating to them when participating in, using or publishing content on any social media site or channel.

Any breach of these rules will be considered a disciplinary matter to be dealt with through the practice's disciplinary procedures.

[Statement or policy example where social media policy is in use]

[Name of practice] uses social media to support our clients and raise awareness of the practice. The social media policy supports our business objectives by [insert objectives support description].

[Name] in [department/unit/team] is responsible for social media for and on behalf of our practice. No other employee or person is authorised to participate in the practice's social media activities without the agreement of [name].

[Name of practice] participates in the following social media site(s): [name(s) of site(s)]. Information posted or viewed on social media sites may constitute published material. Therefore, reproduction of information posted or otherwise available over the internet may only be done by [name(s) or department/team] who [is/are] delegated with authority to do this on behalf of the practice.

Employees must not act in such a way as to breach copyright or the licensing conditions of any internet site or computer programme. Any breach of our social media rules or guidance will be considered a disciplinary matter to be dealt with through the our disciplinary procedures.

Scope

This policy covers all individuals working at all levels and grades, including partners, senior managers, officers, directors, employees, consultants, contractors, trainees, home workers, part-time and fixed-term employees, casual and agency staff and volunteers, collectively referred to as staff in this policy.

Third parties who have access to the practice's electronic communication systems and equipment are also required to comply with this policy.

Relevant social media

This policy deals with the use of all forms of social media, including, though not exclusively and exhaustively:

- Facebook;
- LinkedIn;
- Twitter;
- Wikipedia;
- all other social networking sites and all internet postings, including blogs.

Applicable use

The policy applies to business and personal use of social media whether:

(a) during office hours or otherwise;
(b) it is accessed using the practice's IT facilities and equipment;
(c) it is accessed using equipment belonging to members of staff.

Consequences of breach

Breaching this policy may result in disciplinary action up to and including dismissal. Disciplinary action may be taken regardless of whether the breach is committed during working hours, and regardless of whether the practice's equipment or facilities are used for the purpose of committing the breach.

Any member of staff suspected of committing a breach of this policy will be required to co-operate with the practice's investigation, which may involve handing over relevant passwords and login details.

Staff may be required to remove internet postings which are deemed to constitute a breach of this policy, and failure to comply with such a request may in itself result in disciplinary action.

[Name] has the responsibility for ensuring that any person who may be involved with administration or investigations carried out under this policy receives regular and appropriate training to assist them with these duties.

Responsibility for implementation

[*Name*] has overall responsibility for the effective operation of this policy, but has delegated day-to-day responsibility for its operation to [*name*]. Responsibility for monitoring the operation of this policy lies with [*name*].

Questions regarding the content or application of this policy should be directed to [*name*].

All partners and managers have a responsibility to maintain compliance with this policy by ensuring that all members of staff understand the standards of behaviour expected of them, and by taking action when behaviour falls below what is required. Relevant training will be provided to enable individuals to do this.

Every member of staff has a responsibility to comply with this policy and must ensure that they take the time to read and understand it.

Any misuse of social media should be reported to [*name*].

Compliance with related policies and agreements

Prohibited use and content

Social media should never be used in a way that breaches any of the practice's policies. If an internet post were to breach any of the practice's policies in another forum, it would also breach them in an online forum. For example, partners and staff are prohibited from using social media to:

- breach the practice's electronic information and communications systems policy;
- breach the practice's obligations with respect to the rules of relevant regulatory bodies;
- breach any obligations they may have relating to confidentiality;
- breach the practice's disciplinary rules;
- defame or disparage the organisation or its affiliates, clients, business partners, suppliers, vendors or other stakeholders;
- harass or bully other staff in any way;
- breach the practice's anti-harassment and bullying policy;
- unlawfully discriminate against other staff or third parties;
- breach the practice's equality and diversity policy;
- breach the practice's data protection policy (for example, by disclosing personal information about a colleague online);
- breach any other laws or ethical standards (for example, using social media in a false or misleading way, such as by claiming to be someone other than themselves or by making misleading statements);
- provide references for other individuals on social or professional networking sites, because such references, either positive or negative, can be attributed to the practice, and create legal liability for both the author of the reference and the practice.

Breaches of any of the above policies will be subject to disciplinary action up to and including termination of employment.

Procedure for the business use of social media

Anyone who is required to use social media on behalf of the practice must seek approval for such communication from [*name*], who will ensure that the following conditions are met:

(a) The communication has been approved by the appropriate head of department.
(b) Client confidentiality is maintained.
(c) Any information relating to the practice is accurate, and can be used without breaching or jeopardising the practice's ability to maintain confidentiality of its strategic and business information.
(d) The practice's logo and/or colour scheme(s) is/are used in compliance with practice wide protocols for their use.
(e) The SRA Code of Conduct 2011 and all legislative and regulatory requirements and restrictions are complied with.

The practice will ensure that individuals who are authorised to use social media on its behalf are trained to do so.

Anyone who is contacted for comments about the practice with a view to publication anywhere, including in any social media outlet, must direct the enquiry to [*name*] and only act in accordance with [his/her] subsequent instructions.

Use of social media in recruitment

[*Each practice to delete whichever of the two alternatives given below does not apply.*]

[The practice may use internet searches to perform due diligence on candidates in the course of recruitment. Where this is done, the practice will act in accordance with its data protection and equal and diversity obligations.]

[*OR*]

[The practice does not permit the use of internet searches for recruitment purposes.]

Personal use of social media

[*Practice name*] recognises that employees may wish to participate in or use social media for personal use. No employee must in any way bring the practice, its staff, its existing or prospective clients or third party individuals/entities connected to the practice into disrepute or publish any information, particularly anything confidential or sensitive, relating to them when participating in, using or publishing content on any social media site or channel.

Any breach of our social media rules or guidance will be considered a disciplinary matter to be dealt with through our disciplinary procedures.

Responsible use of social media

Given below are common sense guidelines and recommendations for using social media responsibly and safely.

1. Protecting the practice's business reputation:

    (a) Staff must not post disparaging or defamatory statements about:

         • the practice;
         • the practice's clients;
         • suppliers and vendors;
         • other affiliates and stakeholders.

    (b) Staff must avoid social media communications that might be misconstrued in a way that could damage the practice's business reputation, even indirectly.
    (c) Staff must make it clear in social media postings that they are speaking on their own behalf; write in the first person; and use a personal email address when communicating via social media.
    (d) Staff are personally responsible for what they communicate in social media, and should remember that what they publish might remain available for reading for a long time by anyone, including people inside or outside of the practice, future employers and social acquaintances.
    (e) If any social medial communication discloses affiliation as an employee of the practice, individuals must make it clear that their views do not represent those of the practice. The following phrase must be inserted at the beginning of the communication:

         The views in this posting do not represent the views of my employer.

         Individuals must also ensure that their profiles and any content they post conveys an image similar to that presented to clients and colleagues.

    (f) Comments about sensitive business-related topics, such as the performance of the practice, must not be posted even if it is made clear that individual's views on such topics do not represent those of the practice. They could still damage the practice's reputation.
    (g) Any uncertainty or concern about the appropriateness of any statement or posting, must be discussed with [*name*] prior to use.
    (h) If a member of staff sees content in a social media posting that disparages or reflects poorly on the practice or the practice's stakeholders, they should contact [*name*]. Everyone is responsible for protecting the practice's business reputation.

2. Respecting intellectual property and confidential information:

    (a) Staff must not do anything to jeopardise the practice's business and other confidential information and intellectual property through the use of social media.

(b) Staff must avoid misappropriating or infringing the intellectual property of other companies and individuals, which can create liabilities for the practice, as well as the individual author.

(c) Staff must not use the practice's logos, brand names, slogans or other trademarks, or post any of the practice's confidential or proprietary information without prior written permission.

(d) In order to protect individuals and the practice against liability for copyright infringement, where appropriate, sources of particular information posted or uploaded must be accurately cited. If there are any questions about whether a particular post or upload might violate copyright or a trademark, [*name*] must be consulted before making the communication.

(e) [Staff are not permitted to add business contacts that have been made during the course of their employment to personal social networking accounts, such as Facebook or LinkedIn accounts.]

[*OR*]

[The contact details of business acquaintances made during the course of employment are regarded as the practice's confidential information, and as such, individuals will be required to delete all such details from their personal social networking accounts upon termination of employment.]

[*Each practice to delete whichever of the two alternatives given above does not apply.*]

3. Respecting colleagues, clients, partners and suppliers:

(a) Individuals must not post anything:

(i) that colleagues or the practice's customers, clients, business partners, suppliers, vendors or other stakeholders would find offensive, including discriminatory comments, insults or obscenities;

(ii) relating to colleagues or the practice's clients, business partners, suppliers, vendors or other stakeholders without their written permission.

Monitoring of use

The contents of the practice's IT resources and communications systems are the practice's property. Therefore, staff should have no expectation of privacy in any message, file, data, document, facsimile, telephone conversation, social media post, conversation or message, or any other kind of information or communications transmitted to, received or printed from, or stored or recorded on the practice's electronic information and communications systems.

The practice reserves the right to, and will from time to time, monitor, intercept and review, without further notice, staff activities using the practice's IT resources and communications systems, including, but not limited to, social media postings and activities, in order to ensure that this policy is being complied with, and for legitimate business purposes.

Individuals consent to such monitoring by their acknowledgement of this policy and their use of such resources and systems. This might include, without limitation, the monitoring, interception, accessing, recording, disclosing, inspecting, reviewing, retrieving and printing of transactions, messages, communications, postings, log-ins, recordings and other uses of the systems, as well as keystroke capturing and other network monitoring technologies.

The practice may store copies of such data or communications for a period of time after they are created, and may delete such copies from time to time without notice.

Members of staff must not use the practice's IT resources and communications systems for any matter that they wish to be kept private or confidential from the practice.

Monitoring and review of this policy

[*Name*] will review this policy at least annually to ensure that it:

(a) meets legal requirements;
(b) reflects best practice; and
(c) is in effective use throughout the practice.

Staff are invited to comment on this policy, and to suggest ways in which it might be improved, by contacting [*name*].

5 People management

Lexcel standard	Guidance
5.1 Training plan Practices will have a plan for the training and development of personnel, which must include: (a) the person responsible for the plan; (b) a procedure for an annual review of the plan, to verify it is in effective operation across the practice.	There is a distinct difference between a training plan and a training and development policy. The former outlines the training and development that is required within the practice over the forthcoming period (at least one year), whereas the latter is a document that outlines the approach that the practice is taking to the whole subject of training and development, e.g. ensuring that everyone is trained to their maximum potential and competence. The plan can form part of the policy, e.g. as an appendix that is updated annually. One way of developing a plan is to design a spreadsheet showing the training needs of individuals that are identified during periodic performance management reviews/appraisals, together with dates of activities that have been arranged in order to meet those needs. The learning and development plan template contained in **Annex 5A** is divided into three sections to reflect common requirements within practices. The first part describes continuing and sometimes repeated 'generic' training that practices may deliver to its partners and staff from time to time. Topics that may fall within this part of the plan could include: • anti-money laundering; • bribery and corruption; • equality and diversity; • data protection and information management; • health and safety; • conflicts of interests; • risk management; • client care. The second part of the plan acknowledges the continuing professional development (CPD) that many individuals are required to undertake by their professional bodies. The third part of the plan is designed to highlight the known training requirements that the practice will need to address within the forthcoming year, and many of these are likely to have emanated from individual appraisals/personal development reviews. It is this part that could be documented on a spreadsheet.

Lexcel standard	Guidance
5.2 Person specifications/job descriptions Practices will list the tasks to be undertaken by all personnel within the practice and document the skills, knowledge and experience required for individuals to fulfil their roles satisfactorily, usually in the form of a person specification.	This requirement can be addressed by job descriptions which also contain details of the knowledge, skills and experience needed for individual roles. Some practices have 'generic' job descriptions for roles such as non-partner fee earners, secretaries and other support staff; whereas larger practices often differentiate levels of fee earner through the terms assistant and associate. It is often the case that partners have more bespoke job descriptions, and this will probably be particularly so for those who have fee earning and other roles, e.g. COLP.
5.3 Recruitment procedures Practices will have procedures to deal effectively with recruitment and selection, which must include: (a) the identification of vacancies; (b) the drafting of the job documentation; (c) methods of attracting candidates and applicants; (d) selection methods used; (e) storage, retention and destruction of records; (f) references and ID checking; (g) checking fee earners' disciplinary records.	Common areas that practices overlook to include when drafting their recruitment procedures are: • identifying who drafts the necessary job documentation whenever the procedure is used; • details of how the storage, retention and destruction of recruitment records is achieved. If the records of successful candidates are retained on their individual personnel files following appointment, then this needs to be made clear in the procedure. The retention of records of unsuccessful candidates also needs to be addressed, and guidance for this is provided by the Information Commissioner: **www.ico.org.uk/for_organisations/data_protection/ topic_guides/~/media/documents/library/Data_Protection/ Practical_application/quick_guide_to_the_employment_ practices_code.ashx** • in relation to recruitment records, it is not unusual for practices to overlook the need to ensure that they can produce recruitment records, e.g. interview notes to assessors. A common problem in this respect is the fact that more senior fee earning appointments, e.g. partners, are sometimes made using procedures other than those that are the norm, and interview notes are not always made, or if they are, not always sent to the appropriate individual for storage; • the need to obtain identification, including evidence of an individual's right to work in the UK; • the checking of fee earners' disciplinary records with the appropriate regulatory bodies, e.g. SRA, CLC, CILEX. It is also a requirement for practices to indicate how they destroy recruitment records.

Lexcel standard	Guidance
5.4 Induction Practices will conduct an appropriate induction for all personnel, including those transferring roles within the practice and must cover: (a) management structure and the individual's job responsibilities; (b) terms and conditions of employment; (c) immediate training requirements; (d) key policies.	Many practices use checklists to guide their inductions. It is recommended that inductees are required to sign the checklists, either during the inductions, or at their conclusion. This could assist practices to refute any subsequent claims that certain key areas, e.g. health and safety, were not addressed.
5.5 Staff leaving procedure Practices will have a procedure which details the steps to be followed when a member of staff ceases to be an employee, which must include: (a) the handover of work; (b) exit interviews; (c) the return of company property.	Practices often use checklists to deal with activities that must be undertaken when an individual leaves a practice. If this is the case, a reference to the checklist needs to be made within the manual, thereby making the checklist a part of the procedure.
5.6 Training and development policy Practices must have a training and development policy including: (a) ensuring that appropriate training is provided to personnel within the practice; (b) ensuring that all supervisors and managers receive appropriate training; (c) a procedure to evaluate training; (d) the person responsible for the policy; (e) a procedure for an annual review of the policy, to verify it is in effective operation across the practice.	See guidance under **5.1** above. The former need for a 'process' [which could be unwritten, though observable] for evaluating training has been replaced with the need for a written procedure. This can be satisfied in a number of ways including (the list is not exhaustive): • training evaluation forms; • discussions at appraisals/personal development reviews; • discussions between attendees and their line managers; • the requirement for attendees to present what they have learned to colleagues; • the evaluation of training includes that which is undertaken internally.

Lexcel standard	Guidance
5.7 Performance management policy Practices will have a performance management policy which includes: (a) the practice's approach to performance management; (b) performance review periods and timescales; (c) the person responsible for the policy; (d) a procedure for an annual review of the policy, to verify it is in effective operation across the practice.	This goes further than simply having an appraisal system, although for many practices, appraisals will remain the mainstay for managing the performance of individuals. The practice must describe how it manages individual performance, including that of individuals who are under performing. This could include, where appropriate, disciplinary/competency hearings, in addition to appraisals. If this is the case, then this part of the standard could be addressed by referring to those disciplinary/competency procedures within the policy. There is a need to describe how often activities such as appraisals and performance reviews are conducted, and the standard recognises that there could be more than one format and timescale used for different levels of staff, including partners. All must be conducted at least annually.

For a learning and development plan, see **Annex 5A.**

For a recruitment procedure, see **Annex 5B.**

For a learning and development policy, see **Annex 5C.**

Annex 5A
Learning and development plan

General

This plan is reviewed [*timescale*] by [*name/role*], normally following the annual round of appraisal/performance management reviews. The plan is kept under regular review by [*name*] in order to ensure that, wherever possible, the learning and development needs that have been identified are being met.

(handwritten: Annually / As.)

The plan is divided into three sections and deals with:

(a) periodic generic training that is provided for everyone;
(b) CPD requirements for qualified fee earning and support staff who have to meet the annual learning and development criteria of their professional institutions; and
(c) learning and development that has been identified from any other appropriate source, including (the list is not exhaustive) performance reviews, strategic planning, team/departmental planning and ad hoc occurrences.

1. Generic learning and development

There is a need to ensure that certain training is provided for relevant individuals, and in some cases, for everyone in the practice in respect of the topics listed below (the list is not exhaustive and is subject to periodic review and, if necessary, amendment). [~~Insert any training that is not listed below that the practice considers must be delivered periodically.~~]

- **Equality and diversity** – The practice has statutory and regulatory obligations under equality and diversity legislation, and to that end, will ensure that appropriate training is provided to everyone in the practice at least every [*insert ~~the frequency within which the practice will provide this training. If it is to be included in this year's plan, then say so~~*]. *(handwritten: YEAR.)*
- **Data protection** – Training on this subject, including information management is provided to everyone in the practice at least every [*insert ~~the frequency within which the practice will provide this training. If it is to be included in this year's plan, then say so~~*]. *(handwritten: YEAR)*
- **Prevention of financial crime** – The practice has three main policies and associated procedures intended to avoid its involvement in financial crime, and training will be provided to everyone in the three areas as indicated below:
  - **Anti-money laundering** [*insert the frequency within which the practice will provide this training. If it is to be included in this year's plan, then say so*];
  - **Prevention of mortgage fraud** [*insert the frequency within which the practice will provide this training. If it is to be included in this year's plan, then say so*];
  - **Bribery Act 2010** [*insert the frequency within which the practice will provide this training. If it is to be included in this year's plan, then say so*].

- **Conflicts of interest** – Training on this will be provided [*insert the frequency within which the practice will provide this training. If it is to be included in this year's plan, then say so*].
- **Client care** – Training on this will be provided [*insert the frequency within which the practice will provide this training. If it is to be included in this year's plan, then say so*].
- **Risk management** – Training on this will be provided [*insert the frequency within which the practice will provide this training. If it is to be included in this year's plan, then say so*].
- **Health and safety** – Training on this will be provided [*insert the frequency within which the practice will provide this training. If it is to be included in this year's plan, then say so*].

2. CPD learning and development

The learning and development that has been identified for individuals who belong to professional institutes and organisations that require them to undertake CPD, is documented within their individual learning and development plans, which form part of their appraisal/performance management reviews.

3. Annual learning and development

The table below contains the planned learning and development, other than that highlighted in 1 and 2 above, to take place in the coming year.

Learning need identified	Candidates identified	Method of delivery	Internal or external (if external, name the provider if known)	Timescale	Cost	Date completed

Annex 5B
Recruitment procedure

Procedure purpose

This procedure has been developed and is managed by [*name*] to assist the practice in:

(a) maintaining a consistent approach to the recruitment of partners, fee earners, secretarial and support staff members;
(b) ensuring compliance with legislative and regulatory requirements, in particular, those relating to equality and diversity, and data protection.

The practice will ensure that all recruitment activities comply with its equality and diversity policy which can be found [*insert the location of the policy, or a hyperlink to it*].

Identification of vacancies

Vacancies within the practice are normally identified in one of three ways:

(a) during the business planning process;
(b) when, during the business year, the practice alters or extends its range of services, or it becomes apparent that an unforeseen need to recruit has occurred; and
(c) when a member of staff leaves and, after a staffing review, it is decided that the vacancy has to be filled.

Recruitment documentation

When there is a need to recruit, the requisite job description and person specification will be drafted by [*name*] in consultation with [*name*] and any other relevant persons.

Dealing with applicants

Potential applicants will be identified through any of the following means:

(a) recommendations from existing staff or professional contacts;
(b) adverts in professional and local newspapers and periodicals;
(c) 'cold' approaches to the practice from suitably qualified people; and
(d) informal approaches by senior members of the practice to individuals who are considered to be potentially suitable for the position in question.
(e) recruitment agencies

When applications are received, they will be reviewed by [*name*], and a shortlist drawn up of people to be invited for interview.

Selection of appointees

Appointees will be selected through:

- a review of their application papers, including CVs or application forms;
- a formal interview with [*name or position*], during which criterion-based questions will be asked in order to ascertain individuals' knowledge, experience, and approach. During these interviews, detailed notes will be taken and retained (see below). It is essential that these notes are comprehensive and are made even for the appointment of senior fee earners, including partners; and
- appropriate references being taken up.

[[It is/It is not] anticipated that medical examinations will form part of the recruitment process.]

[OR]

[*Insert the practice's procedures for obtaining medical examinations if that is relevant to the procedure that the practice uses.*]

All recruitment documentation, including notes from interviews, will be confidentially retained as follows, in line with the Employment Practice Code of the Information Commissioner:

- successful applicants – documents will be retained in their personal files for the duration of their employment with the practice, and six months beyond, following which period they will be confidentially shredded;
- unsuccessful applicants – documents will be retained for six months in line with the Employment Practice Code of the Information Commissioner. Following this period, they will be confidentially shredded.

Additional applicant information

When it has been decided to appoint an individual, where possible prior to the offer of appointment, the following information will be obtained from the appointee; or if that is not possible, it will be made known to the individual that the appointment is made subject to the practice satisfactorily obtaining the following information:

- personal identification through some form of photographic evidence, e.g. passport or driving licence, together with evidence of address;
- evidence of the individual's right to work in the UK through official documents or enquiries with the appropriate agencies; and
- with regard to fee-earners, details of their disciplinary records through bodies such as the SRA, CILEx and CLC.

At the end of any probationary period, it will not be possible to confirm an appointment until this information has been obtained.

Review

This procedure will be reviewed at least annually by [*name*] to ensure that it is being consistently operated throughout the practice.

Annex 5C
Learning and development policy

Policy statement

It is the policy of the practice to ensure that everyone maintains appropriate levels of competence and knowledge in order that the practice can provide informed and sound advice to its clients, and that support functions operate effectively, efficiently and safely. [*Name*] is responsible for the development, review and management of this policy.

It is also the policy of the practice that, wherever possible, individuals will be encouraged to develop their knowledge and skills in pursuit of career aspirations that are relevant to the practice; and if sufficient resources are available, consideration will be given to providing financial and other assistance for them to do so.

Scope

This policy applies to all individuals working at every level and grade, including partners, senior managers, officers, directors, employees, consultants, contractors, trainees, home workers, part-time and fixed-term employees, casual and agency staff and volunteers, collectively referred to as staff in this policy.

Identification of learning requirements

Learning and development requirements for individuals, teams, and the practice are identified from a number of sources including (the list is not exhaustive):

(a)   the business planning process;
(b)   appraisals and other performance management reviews that may be undertaken; and
(c)   informal observations and discussions between individuals and their managers.

Forms of learning and development

The practice recognises that learning and development is not confined to formal courses and seminars, and is often most valuable when undertaken in the workplace through coaching and other training given by colleagues and line managers. Such learning activities are encouraged and valued by the practice.

Management and supervisory training

The practice recognises the important roles that managers and supervisors have in the day-to-day management and control of the practice. Although the practice complies with the requirements of the SRA Practice Framework Rules 2011 and will ensure that it always does so, it intends that all individuals in fee earning and support staff management or supervisory positions will, where appropriate, receive training relevant to their management and supervisory responsibilities.

This training will not be confined to formal courses, although these will always be considered where appropriate. Much of the training is likely to comprise on-the-job coaching and mentoring of individuals by experienced managers and supervisors.

The practice will ensure that, individuals who are nominated as supervisors for publicly funded work, comply with the requirements for supervision training under that contract.

Management and supervisory skills form part of the appraisal/performance management reviews of those who hold such positions, and where a need for learning and development relevant to management and supervision is identified, the procedure that is described below under 'Applying for learning and development' will be followed.

Learning and development planning

When learning and development needs are identified, they are put into the practice's training plan, and, in the case of individuals, their personal training plans.

Applying for learning and development

When learning and development needs have been identified, individuals will complete a 'learning and development application and planning' form and submit it through their line manager to [name], who has overall responsibility for learning AS, and development within the practice.

[Name] will, where possible, approve the learning and development activity, AS following which it will be the responsibility of the individual concerned and their line manager to identify an appropriate provider of the activity required and make arrangements for the individual to attend. [Name] will be informed when the AS necessary arrangements have been made, in order that the practice's training plan can be updated, and appropriate resources allocated.

Evaluation of learning and development

It is important that all learning and development, regardless of how it is undertaken, is evaluated, and this is achieved through various means including (the list is not exhaustive):

(a) discussion at appraisal and other performance development meetings;
(b) informal discussions between individuals and line managers;
(c) where appropriate, individuals providing presentations to colleagues;
(d) completion of the evaluation part of the learning and development application and planning form which must be used following all learning and development activities. These forms are collated by [name] who retains them centrally.   PM

PM

Where it has been identified that a learning and development activity has been unsatisfactory, [*name*] will be informed, and the activity provider contacted in order to give them feedback and, where it is felt appropriate, obtain some form of rebate of the fees paid.

Monitoring and review

k

[*Name*] is responsible for monitoring this policy, and will conduct a review of its operation and effectiveness at least annually. The outcomes of the reviews will be recorded.

Learning and development application and planning		
Delegate:		
Course title:		
Date(s):		
CPD points:		
Costs		
Travel:	**Tutor/course fees:**	
Accommodation:	**Other:**	
	Total cost:	
What are the delegate's objectives for the training/development? 1. 2. 3.		
Which individual/team/departmental/practice objective(s) is this learning/development activity targeting? 1. 2. 3.		
Date set for evaluation meeting:		
Delegate's signature:	**Date:**	
Manager's signature:	**Date:**	
Request/application approved/not approved:	Approved ☐ Not approved ☐	
Signed:		
Date:		

Learning and development evaluation
Did the learning/development meet the desired objectives?
If not, please describe the shortcomings:
What usable benefits did the delegate obtain from the activity? 1. 2. 3. 4. 5.
Is any follow up action required? (If so, please briefly describe)
Are there any comments/issues with regard to the learning/development provider?
Delegate's signature: Date: Manager's signature: Date:

6 Risk management

Lexcel standard	Guidance
6.1 Risk manager Practices must designate one overall risk manager to be able to identify and deal with all risk issues which may arise.	The risk manager must be someone who has sufficient authority to deal with risk issues and appropriate decisions that may occur and be required.
6.2 Named supervisors There will be a named supervisor for each area of work undertaken by the practice.	Many practices deal with this through organisational charts.
6.3 Managing high risk matters Practices must have procedures to manage instructions which may be undertaken even though they have a higher risk profile, including unusual supervisory and reporting requirements or contingency planning.	It is accepted that practices cannot operate in a 'risk free' environment, but in acknowledging this fact, the standard requires them to establish a system of reporting high risk matters, preferably to the risk manager.
6.4 Work lists and work refusals Practices must maintain lists of work that the practice will and will not undertake. This information must be communicated to all relevant staff and must be updated when changes occur.	Lists of work that the practice will and will not undertake must be developed. While it is accepted that these lists could be very long, it is normal for practices to deal with this by providing headings of matter types, e.g. domestic conveyancing, corporate, wills and probate.
6.5 Generic risk lists Practices must maintain details of the generic risks and causes of claims associated with the area(s) of work undertaken by the practice. This information must be communicated to all relevant staff.	There are two risk lists required. The first comprises details of risks that are generic regardless of the type of matter, for example (the list is not exhaustive): • matters that have been brought by clients from other practices; • clients based outside of the UK; • clients with a poor record for paying bills; • matters with imminent limitation or key hearing dates; • matters, the actual or potential values of which are close to, or exceed, the practice's professional indemnity insurance limit; The second list(s) comprises details of risks and causes of complaints in relation to the different types of matter that a practice may undertake. Examples of these are provided within this toolkit.

Lexcel standard	Guidance
6.6 Defining key dates Practices must document key dates, including: (a) the definition of key dates by work type; (b) [a system to ensure that] key dates [are] recorded on the file and in a back up system.	There is a tendency for practices to sometimes give 'typical' examples of key dates without actually creating definitive lists. It is the latter that is required by the standard. Many practices now include these key dates in their lists of generic risks.
6.7 Monitoring key dates Practices must have a procedure to monitor key dates to reduce the risk of key dates being missed.	Hitherto, practices have been required to have a process for the monitoring of key dates, but now there must be a documented procedure to be followed by everyone.
6.8 Conflicts of interests policy Practices will have a policy on the handling of conflicts, which must include: (a) the definition of conflicts by work type; (b) training for all relevant personnel to identify conflicts; (c) steps to be followed when a conflict is identified; (d) the person responsible for the policy; (e) a procedure for an annual review of the policy, to verify it is in effective operation across the practice.	Practices must have a clear policy to deal with conflicts of interests, and must define what they consider to be conflicts of interests within each type of matter that they undertake. Having identified what conflicts there may be, the policy must also describe the actions to be taken when conflicts have been identified. With regard to training, relevant personnel could include secretaries, or members of accounts departments, who may be involved in conducting conflicts of interests searches.
6.9 Active supervision Practices will have a procedure to ensure that all personnel, both permanent and temporary, are actively supervised. Such procedures will include: (a) checks on incoming and outgoing correspondence, where appropriate; (b) departmental, team and office meetings and communication structures; (c) reviews of matter details in order to ensure good financial controls and the appropriate allocation of workloads; (d) the exercise of devolved powers in publicly funded work; (e) the availability of a supervisor; (f) allocation of new work and reallocation of existing work, if necessary.	All previous versions of the standard have referred to processes for supervision, but now practices must document supervision procedures that cover the areas mentioned in this part of the standard. This will involve describing activities that most practices have probably been undertaking for years without formally recording them.
6.10 Checking for inactivity Practices will have a procedure to ensure that all those doing legal work check their files regularly for inactivity.	Formerly the standard required a process for inactivity checking, but now there must be a procedure to deal with this issue.

Lexcel standard	Guidance
6.11 File reviews Practices will have a procedure for regular, independent file reviews, of either the management of the file or its substantive legal content, or both. In relation to file reviews, practices will: • define file selection criteria; • define the number and frequency of reviews; • retain a record of the file review on the matter file and centrally; • ensure any corrective action which is identified in a file review is acted upon within 28 days and verified by the reviewer; • ensure that the designated supervisor reviews and monitors the data generated by file reviews; • conduct a review at least annually of the data generated by file reviews.	The annual review must be documented, but practices need to be aware of the provision requiring supervisors to monitor data from file reviews on an ongoing basis. Although the standard does not specifically say that the outcomes of these ongoing reviews and monitoring must be documented, it is suggested that there is benefit to be gained from their documentation and subsequent reporting to appropriate people, such as the risk manager and/or departmental heads.
6.12 Risk assessments Operational risk will be considered and recorded in all matters before, during and after the processing of instructions. Before the matter is undertaken the fee earners must: (a) consider if a new client and/or matter should be accepted by the practice, in accordance with section 8.1 [of the standard]; (b) assess the risk profile of all new instructions and notify the risk manager in accordance with procedures under 6.3 of any unusual or high risk considerations in order that appropriate action may be taken. During the retainer the fee earner must: (c) consider any change to the risk profile of the matter and report and advise on such circumstances without delay, informing the risk manager if appropriate; (d) inform the client in all cases where an adverse costs order is made against the practice in relation to the matter in question. At the end of the matter the fee earner must: (e) undertake a concluding risk assessment by considering if the client's objectives have been achieved; (f) notify the risk manager of all such circumstances [where client objectives have not been achieved, or risk issues remain in the matter] in accordance with documented procedures.	Not only do risk assessments have to be conducted, they must also be recorded; an activity that many practices address by using a File Summary Sheet. Some practices have a specific risk assessment form that is used for this purpose. The standard does not require a documented procedure to ensure that these risk assessments are undertaken, but many practices do have such procedures. There is sometimes confusion in respect of initial risk assessments, because it is not unusual for fee earners to consider this as part of the anti-money laundering (AML) Client Due Diligence (CDD) risk assessment; but it is not. It is a completely different assessment designed to examine the operational risks associated with the matter. Although fee earners and supervisors are required to monitor risk levels of matters, the outcomes of the ongoing monitoring do not need to be documented unless the risk level of a matter has changed (increased), in which case this fact must be documented, and if necessary, reported to an appropriate person, e.g. the risk manager. The closing risk assessment is sometimes recorded on a file closure checklist that a number of practices use.

Lexcel standard	Guidance
6.13 Annual risk analyses Practices will analyse at least annually all risk assessment data generated within the practice. This must include: (a) any indemnity insurance claims (where applicable); (b) an analysis of client complaints trends; (c) data generated by file reviews; (d) the identification of remedial action [required as a result of the review].	This is an annual report on the analysis of information from the various sources indicated by this part of the standard. A common addition to the list is an analysis of client satisfaction levels. Although not specifically required by the standard, it is considered useful for the report to be contained in one document compiled by the risk manager. In many practices, heads of departments are required to compile similar reports which they then give to risk manager, who summarises their content and the trends identified therein for the information and consideration of senior individuals and bodies within the practices.
6.14 Prevention of financial crime Practices will have procedures for the prevention of financial crime, including: (a) the person responsible for the procedure; (b) a documented review of the procedures at least annually, to verify they are in effective operation across the practice.	The areas that must be addressed as a minimum are: • anti-money laundering; • the prevention of mortgage fraud; • the Bribery Act 2010.

Risk must be an integral theme throughout any practice's management framework. Key components of risk within legal practices include:

- responsibility at, and support from, senior management level;
- a framework for managing risk across all parts of the business;
- integration of risk management processes into everything the practice does;
- accountability in each practice area and all support functions;
- open lines of communication to support the review and updating of risks;
- regular review, evaluation and assessment of risks;
- business continuity planning and testing.

Without these elements, practices risk jeopardising the success of implementing an effective risk management or quality system. In particular, regular reviews will help maximise the relevance of the framework for your practice, making sure you are trying to mitigate appropriate risks. The ramifications of not completing regular and thorough risk analysis can be significant for any practice – from minor mistakes, to loss of business.

For a policy on day-to-day operational supervision, see **Annex 6A**.

For an independent file review procedure, see **Annex 6B**.

Examples of generic risk profiles (see 6.5 of the Lexcel standard) are given in **Annex 6C**.

An example of a generic risk table is given at **Annex 6D**.

A conflicts of interests policy (see 6.8 of the Lexcel standard) is given at **Annex 6E**.

A policy on financial crime is given at **Annex 6F** (see 6.14 of the Lexcel standard). A separate, more detailed anti-bribery and corruption policy is given at **Annex 6G**.

Annex 6A
Procedures relating to day-to-day supervision

General statement

[*Name*] is responsible for developing, monitoring and managing this procedure. The procedures described below deal with day-to-day operational supervision, and must be read in conjunction with other policies and procedures including (list is not exhaustive):

- accepting and declining instructions;
- client care;
- risk management;
- conflicts of interests;
- financial crime;
- procedures designed to ensure compliance with the SRA Handbook;
- outsourcing;
- time recording;
- financial transactions and billing.

Scope

These procedures apply to all individuals working at every level and grade, including partners, senior managers, officers, directors, employees, consultants, contractors, trainees, home workers, part-time and fixed-term employees, casual and agency staff and volunteers, collectively referred to as staff in this policy.

Application

These procedures deal with the following areas of supervision:

- incoming and outgoing post;
- meetings;
- reviews of the conduct of matters;
- the exercise of devolved powers in publicly funded work;
- the availability of supervisors;
- the allocation and reallocation of work;
- prevention of inactivity.

Correspondence and emails

[*Fully describe how the practice deals with incoming and outgoing correspondence.*

Points to consider:

- *How is incoming post dealt with?*
- *What arrangements exist for the monitoring of outgoing post, e.g. do all fee earners or those with less than 'x' years post-qualified experience (PQE) have to show outgoing post that provides advice to a supervisor beforehand?*
- *How are outgoing emails dealt with, particularly those that provide advice, and those sent by fee earners with less than 'x' years PQE?*]

Meetings

[*Fully describe the meeting structures that exist within the practice. Everyone, including support and secretarial staff must be involved in meetings during the year, although the nature and frequency is a matter for the practice.*

Points to consider:

- *How often do departmental and/or team meetings take place?*
- *What meetings, and with what frequency, are held for support staff?*
- *Are there any one-to-one meetings between supervisors and fee earners? If so, how frequently, and what do they deal with?*
- *Are there any 'whole practice' or 'whole office' meetings? If so, how frequent are they?*
- *What other meetings are there: e.g. marketing, risk, strategy, partners, board, etc.?*]

Matter reviews

[*Describe exactly the practice's procedures for reviewing matters, other than formal file reviews.*

Points to consider:

- *Does the practice have monthly printouts issued to all fee earners about which they are expected to comment or report to their supervisors about the current situation with regard to their matters?*
- *Are there any monthly or other periodic meetings on a one-to-one basis between fee earners and their supervisors, during which matters are discussed?*
- *Describe what, if any, information is provided to supervisors in order that they can monitor the types and levels of work for the fee earners within their teams?*
- *Describe what, if any, other systems and procedures the practice has to review current matters and examine workloads?*]

Devolved powers

[*If the practice has a CLA contract, describe exactly how it exercises devolved powers.*]

Availability of supervisors

It is important that the practice ensures the availability of supervisors to provide guidance to, and the supervision of, fee earners when requested or required. In order to maintain the necessary supervision, [*describe exactly the procedures that the practice has in place to ensure that a relevant supervisor is always available for consultation by fee earners*].

[*Points to consider:*

- *What arrangements are made for fee earners to be able to contact supervisors when there are none available on the premises?*
- *What requirements are made on supervisors to ensure that their supervisees know how and where to contact them?*]

Allocation and reallocation of work

[*Describe exactly how work is allocated within the practice.*

Points to consider:

- *It may be that the allocation and reallocation of work is linked to the procedures identified above for monitoring matters.*
- *It is likely that there will be a close relationship between this procedure and the one relating to the Acceptance and Declining of Instructions.*
- *Who makes the decision to allocate work?*]

[*Describe exactly what the procedure is to reallocate work when necessary.*

Points to consider:

- *What criteria are used to reallocate work?*
- *When work is reallocated, what information is provided to ensure that the new fee earner is accurately recorded against the matter?*
- *Do not forget the requirement of 8.3 of the Lexcel standard, which requires that clients will be informed in writing if the person with conduct of their matter changes.*]

Prevention of matter inactivity

The practice acknowledges that one of the biggest sources of complaints from clients is the lack of communication and updating in respect of their matters. There is also a substantial risk of claims if fee earners do not maintain a system of monitoring their matters closely to ensure that important dates are recorded, backed up and met, and that matters are progressed as quickly as possible. In order to minimise these risks, the following procedure(s) will be strictly observed by all fee earners.

[Describe exactly what fee earners are expected to do in order to ensure that matters do not become unnecessarily inactive.

Points to consider:

- *Are fee earners expected to conduct cabinet reviews periodically? If they are, are they required to make a report to anyone that they have done so, and at the same time indicate matters which have been inactive for a period of time, e.g. two months, three months, etc.?*
- *Do fee earners receive regular printouts of the financial status of their current matters, to include details of when an activity last occurred on each matter?*
- *Fully describe any other procedure or procedures that the practice has to ensure that inactivity is prevented.]*

Annex 6B
Independent file review procedure

Independent file reviews are seen by the practice as a major part of its operational risk management strategy. It is also obvious that the SRA sees these reviews as an important part of supervision (please see SRA Authorisation Rules 2011, rule 8, guidance note (iii)).

The practice operates a system of independent file reviews that are conducted as described below. The reviews will be conducted by people other than the fee earners who are managing the selected matters on a day-to-day basis.

Choosing the files

[*Points to consider:*

- *The files will be selected at random, or using other criteria that the practice may wish to apply, e.g.:*

  - *high risk matters;*
  - *files that have been inactive for a period of time;*
  - *files covering the range of matters that a fee earner undertakes;*
  - *files that appear to have high levels of work in progress (WIP) on them.*

- *The selection could be made from a monthly printout of current matters for each fee earner.*
- *The selection could be purely at random with no other criteria.*
- *Some practices have a system whereby the secretary of the reviewer simply goes to the reviewee's cabinet and selects files.*]

The files to be reviewed will be selected by [*indicate exactly how they will be selected, and by whom*]. Under no circumstances will the fee earners with day-to-day conduct of the matters make the selection as to which of their files will be reviewed.

What will be reviewed

The nature of the review will be to examine [*indicate whether the reviews will concentrate on the legal advice, or the compliance and administration of the file or both*].

The reviewers

[*Indicate who will be the authorised reviewers of matter files. If the review will include the quality of legal advice, then the reviewer must be someone with sufficient competency and experience in the relevant area of law. Many practices simply examine the administrative and compliance aspect of files, leaving the quality of advice to be discussed in other forums, e.g. one-to-one meetings between fee earners and supervisors.*]

Frequency of reviews

[*Points to consider:*

- *The frequency must be sufficient to demonstrate an effective system. It is highly unlikely that one or two files per fee earner per annum will be considered sufficient, regardless of the level of fee earner.*
- *A common frequency is one file per fee earner per month, or variations of this, e.g. three files per fee earner per quarter.*
- *Some practices have differing numbers of files reviewed, dependent on the experience of the fee earners, e.g. fee earners with <'x' years post-qualified experience (PQE) will have 'y' number of files examined per month; fee earners with >'x' years PQE will have 'z' number of files examined per month.*]

[*Indicate how often the file reviews will be undertaken, and how many files per fee earner will be seen.*]

Records

Reviewers will use the file review form [*indicate where in the manual or on the intranet the form can be found*].

Every question and area on the file review form will be completed, and whenever the answer to a section or question is 'No', there will be the need for a corrective action to be undertaken.

If there is a need for corrective action:

- the reviewer will clearly indicate what needs to be done in order to make the file compliant;
- the exact date of the review will be put onto the form, and the details of the required corrective actions will be signed and dated by the reviewer;
- the reviewer will retain a copy of the form, and another copy will be placed onto the file that has been reviewed [*indicate where on the file the form should be placed, e.g. on the inside cover, or in sequence with other correspondence in the main body of the file*];
  (*N.B. It is known that some professional indemnity (PI) insurers are concerned about copies of file review forms being retained on matter files. The Lexcel standard requires that a record of the review needs to be kept on the matter file concerned, but this can be in the form of a note indicating that the review has taken place, together with the date of the review. This note can be made on, for example, any file summary sheet that is used.*)
- the fee earner will undertake the required corrective actions, and these must be completed within 28 days of the review;

- when the required corrective actions have been completed, the fee earner will sign and date the file review form to say that the actions have been finalised, and then pass the form to the reviewer;
- the reviewer will then examine the file to ensure that the corrective actions have been fully completed, and then sign and date the form to confirm that the file is now compliant;
- the form will then be copied, and placed on the matter file [see warning note regarding PI insurers above];
- the reviewer will then send the completed form to [indicate to whom the form should be sent, e.g. COLP, risk manager];
- [name] will maintain a central register of all completed file reviews.

Analysis of data

One of the main reasons for file reviews is to identify some or all of the following:

(a) good practice;
(b) potential complaints or claims;
(c) training needs for individuals;
(d) actual or potential trends of non-compliance on the part of either individual fee earners or departments as a whole.

[Person who retains the central register of file reviews, or other relevant individual] will examine all of the data from the file reviews throughout the practice at least [indicate how often this will be done, e.g. following each round of reviews; or monthly; or quarterly; or biannually]. Following these reviews, a report will be submitted to [the partners/executive committee/board/management committee/risk and compliance/other person or body to whom these reports will be submitted].

In addition to these periodic reviews, [name of person who retains the central record of the file reviews or other relevant individual] will examine all of the file review data annually and submit a report to [the partners/executive committee/ board/management committee/risk and compliance committee/other person or body to whom these reports will be submitted]. This report will form part of the annual review of risk.

Review

These procedures will be reviewed annually by [name] and a report will be submitted to [the partners/executive committee/board/management committee/risk and compliance committee/other person or body to whom these reports will be submitted].

Any amendments to these procedures will be notified to all members of the practice, and where it is considered appropriate, training will be provided for those affected by the amendments.

Annex 6C

Example generic risk profiles

Introduction

This document contains examples of generic risks that can occur in different areas of legal work. The risks are contained within various common categories, and they are not to be regarded as exhaustive, and are intended to be regularly reviewed and amended and/or extended as required, based on working experiences.

The following statement applies to each category of risk:

The factors that are described are invariably present in this area of work, and need to be considered at all times. If these factors are not properly addressed, they may result in risks materialising, with consequences that could lead to complaints and/or negligence claims.

Residential property

The main areas risks associated with dealing with residential property work are:

1. *Professional negligence*

(a) Identification of defects in title.
(b) Reporting to mortgagees matters that might affect their decision to proceed with the loan.
(c) Understanding the impact of legislation or case law on a particular set of circumstances.
(d) Complying with time limits for securing priority of buyers and mortgagees and stamping and registration of documents.
(e) Reporting to clients the results of all investigations of title.

2. *Breaches of professional codes of conduct*

(a) Supplying sufficient costs information to clients at the outset of a transaction.
(b) Supplying details of terms and conditions of business.
(c) Supplying details of complaints procedures.
(d) Recognising the occasions where a professional undertaking may be required and obtaining the appropriate authority to give such an undertaking.
(e) Complying with either express or implied undertakings.
(f) Identifying actual or potential conflicts of interests.

3. *Failure to recover all or part of our fees*

(a) Timing of delivery of bill of costs.
(b) Requesting adequate funds prior to completion of the transaction.
(c) Correct calculation of funds required from clients.
(d) Advising clients of change in circumstances requiring revision of estimate/ quote.
(e) Assessing the likely cost to the practice of undertaking a particular matter.

4. *Money laundering*

(a) Receipt of unusual instructions regarding the acceptance and transmission of funds.
(b) Receipt of unexpected or larger than expected sums of money.
(c) Receipt of cash.
(d) Failure to notify suspicions of money laundering to the money laundering reporting officer (MLRO).

5. *Mortgage fraud*

Compliance with the Law Society practice note: Mortgage fraud.

Types of matters that are likely to fall within acceptable risk levels

(a) Acting for either buyer or seller in a transactional sale or purchase between parties at arms length for market value.
(b) Granting long leases for a premium.
(c) Preparing short term tenancies for landlords or approving the same for tenants.
(d) Acting for one party in effecting a transfer following matrimonial proceedings.
(e) Acting for executors in the transfer of property following death of the owner.

Types of matters that are likely to fall outside acceptable risk levels

(a) Acting for both parties in a transaction.
(b) Transactions that involve complex or esoteric points of law outside of usual types of instruction.
(c) Accepting instructions from one of multiple owners purporting to have authority to give instructions on behalf of all owners.
(d) Transfers of property where money is not passing through our account or the account of another solicitor in a chain of transactions.

Employment law

The main areas risks associated with dealing with employment work are:

1.   Professional negligence

(a) Time limit: claims must be brought within three months from the effective date of termination (EDT) bearing in mind the 28-day requirement in respect of some grievances under the statutory rules.

(b) Reasons for bringing a claim: necessity to consider, when acting for employer, whether the employee, in ostensibly complaining about e.g. unfair dismissal, actually also has another underlying complaint which should be dealt with under the statutory grievance procedure. This applies of course also if acting for an employee, in which situation it is necessary to advise them on the grievance procedure.

(c) Clients should be advised where appropriate of latest legislation given the constant deluge, thus failing to advise the client (whether employer or employee) on a particular legal point could lead to a claim or at least criticism. It is important that terms are not inconsistent with current legislation, e.g. with contracts for employer clients.

(d) When acting for employee, failing to take into account or get instructions on all his or her potential losses for purposes of compensation.

(e) Acting on matters where insufficient experience, e.g. trade union matters.

(f) Failing to advise employee client of other potential forms of funding, e.g. household insurance.

2.   Breaches of professional code of conduct

It is necessary to check when a client books an appointment that we do not also act for the other party. With employment matters it is perhaps more likely that an employee will both live and work in this area and therefore there is a higher risk that we will also act for the employer (or the other way round).

3.   Money laundering

(a) Receipt of unexpected or larger than expected sums of money on account of costs or otherwise.

(b) Receipt of cash.

(c) Failure to notify suspicions of money laundering to the MLRO.

Types of matters that are likely to fall outside acceptable risk levels

Inevitably there are in employment law always matters which are new or which do not fall neatly within existing realms of experience. Therefore with each new matter there should be consideration of whether it is in the existing knowledge or easily accessible research resources of the fee earner. Further, even within familiar areas, it is necessary to ensure that the full complexity of the matter is appreciated, e.g. some discrimination claims can be extremely complex.

If it is for an existing client where one is reluctant to say it is outside one's experience in case they go elsewhere and stay there, then where necessary use counsel, perhaps more than one normally would, if necessary paying for the advice as a department expense, as a means of improving one's knowledge: treat as an additional resource in the same way as books and other literature are used. Also, for complex and lengthy advocacy (e.g. for final hearings) counsel should be used, in any event, as in general litigation matters. There may be (as there has already been) cases where publicity is likely to ensue.

Procedures to manage cases falling outside acceptable risk levels

(a) Details of all cases likely to fall outside acceptable risk levels must be given to [*name*] by means of a short written synopsis of the factors and followed by a discussion with [him/her]. This must occur at the outset of taking instructions.
(b) If it is decided to take the matter on, details will be supplied to the overall risk manager for the practice.
(c) Non-director fee earners to report at one-monthly intervals to [*name*] unless or until instructed that reports at shorter or longer intervals are required.
(d) Failing to advise on the cost/benefit to client. This is perhaps particularly important in employment matters because if the matter goes to a tribunal there are no costs awards made except in exceptional circumstances. Therefore, when acting for an employee client, they need to be aware that any monies that they may recover may be eaten into by any costs. Perhaps consider offering to run the claim on a contingency fee basis: as employment matters are regarded as being non-contentious work (even when there is a dispute involved), this is the only form of legal work in this country where it is possible to act on a contingency fee basis. Consult with [*name*] before taking on any client on this basis as it will be necessary to have the client sign a particular agreement.

Selling or buying a business being a sale by way of transfer of assets (not including a sale of shares)

The main risks associated with dealing with these types of work are:

1. Professional negligence

(a) Identification of details in title including freeholds and in particular the provisions and terms of any lease to be acquired where acting for a buyer. In-depth advice as to the implications of the lease being assigned, if any, where acting for a buyer.
(b) Advising on the split of the purchase price generally between goodwill, property and fixtures and fittings and informing the clients that the best advice they should obtain is from their accountant.
(c) Advising on VAT and again informing clients that they should obtain advice from their accountant rather than us, making certain that the client obtains such advice in writing.
(d) Dealing with any particular licences including drink and betting office licences.
(e) Advising on employees and in this instance it is better to ask our counsel to so advise.

(f)   Making certain that fixtures and fittings are not subject to any higher purchase/
rental or the like.

(g)   Where acting for the sale and making certain that any continuing personal
obligations (e.g. guarantee on a machine) are discharged at completion or
novated.

(h)   Advising on the position regarding work in progress, if any, and the
arrangements for splitting the same between the buyer and the seller.

(i)   Advising on the implications of any restrictive covenant required by the seller
not to compete in the future.

(j)   Where funding is required for a purchase, advising the lender on all matters
that might affect their decision to proceed and obtaining written confirmation
before exchange of contracts, in particular advising the client if security is
required from any other source such as the buyer's own home. Dealing with all
appropriate re-mortgage documents for the same including local searches.
Confirming to the client in writing by way of proper report on all matters and
in particular those of complexity and uncertainty.

2.   Breaches of professional codes of conduct

(a)   Supplying sufficient costs information to clients at the outset of a transaction.

(b)   Supplying details of terms and conditions of business.

(c)   Supplying details of complaints procedures.

(d)   Recognising the occasions where a professional undertaking may be required
and obtaining the appropriate authority to give such an undertaking.

(e)   Complying with either express or implied undertakings.

(f)   Identifying actual or potential conflicts of interests.

3.   Failure to recover all or part of our fees

(a)   Timing of delivery of bill of costs.

(b)   Requesting adequate funds prior to completion of the transaction.

(c)   Correct calculation of funds required from clients.

(d)   Advising clients of change in circumstances requiring revision of estimate/
quote.

(e)   Assessing the likely cost to the practice of undertaking a particular matter.

4.   Money laundering

(a)   Receipt of unusual instructions regarding the acceptance and transmission of
funds.

(b)   Receipt of unexpected or larger than expected sums of money.

(c)   Receipt of cash.

(d)   Failure to notify suspicions of money laundering to the MLRO.

5. *Mortgage fraud*

Compliance with the Law Society practice note: Mortgage fraud.

Types of matters that are likely to all within acceptable risk levels

Acting for the buyer and the lender although careful consideration must always be given as it is often better to decline to act for the lender on commercial matters unless the purchase is very straightforward. This is partly because most lenders do not have any apparent and specific requirements in regard to their instructions.

Types of matters that are likely to fall outside acceptable risk levels

(a) Acting for a seller and buyer.
(b) Acting for both parties in a transaction.
(c) Acting for a lender where the transaction is substantial or complex or where the lender's instructions are not clear or where the lender is not a well known and established lender such as a clearing bank.
(d) Acting for two sellers if they are in conflict in which case one must instruct other solicitors.
(e) Impossible time limits where it is virtually impossible to properly and fully investigate the document where we act for a buyer in which event we must obtain written confirmation from the buyer as to the limit of our responsibilities.
(f) Acting for more than one buyer where those buyers may be in conflict.
(g) Acting where particular unusual licences or requirements are needed outside our own personal knowledge in regard to the business concerned unless the buyer limits our responsibilities, e.g. health and safety aspects in buying an old person's residential home.

General litigation matters

The main risks associated with litigation work are:

1. *Professional negligence*

    (a) Failure to meet time limits, particularly relating to:

        (i)   pre-action protocol requirements;
        (ii)   starting of proceedings and giving of notices;
        (iii)   dealing with procedural directions;
        (iv)   hearing dates;
        (v)   appeals.

    (b) Delay and lack of sufficient communication causing risk of:

        (i)   prejudice to client's case;
        (ii)   client complaint;
        (iii)   costs reduction on assessment or by need to accommodate client

concerns;

    (iv)   adverse procedural orders or striking out for want of prosecution or non-compliance.

(c) Complexity of the law, including:

    (i)   availability of up-to-date resources which need to be accessed;
    (ii)   variety of matters within the ambit of litigation work;
    (iii)   assessment of potential outcomes and chances of success.

(d) Administration of advice to client, including assessment of:

    (i)   the need for advice and assistance from experts and counsel;
    (ii)   alternative funding arrangements;
    (iii)   cost/benefit to client;
    (iv)   estimated future costs and updating thereof;
    (v)   quality of historic evidence (where relevant);
    (vi)   quality of consultants and of evidence;
    (vii) probability of success;
    (viii) possibility of costs being awarded against client;
    (ix)   desirability of alternative dispute resolution procedures.

2.   Breaches of professional codes of conduct

(a) Identifying actual or potential conflicts of interests bearing in mind that the practice may have acted for other affected parties.
(b) Supplying sufficient costs information at the outset of a transaction, particularly where the course the matter will follow is unknown at that time.
(c) Updating on costs information.
(d) Generally complying with requirements for client care.

3.   Failure to recover all or part of our fees

(a) Requesting money on account at inception and appropriate stages in a matter, particularly where disbursements are incurred.
(b) Prompt delivery of bills of costs on an interim and final basis.
(c) Explanation of the limitations on costs recovery from opposing party.

4.   Money laundering

(a) Receipt of unusual instructions regarding the acceptance and transmission of funds.
(b) Receipt of unexpected or larger than expected sums of money on account of costs or otherwise.
(c) Receipt of cash.
(d) Failure to notify suspicions of money laundering to the MLRO.

Cases outside acceptable risk levels

(a) [*Matters outside the categories allocated to individual fee earners in the annexed allocation of litigation work*].
(b) All cases where the risk to the client of failure is known or suspected to exceed £1 million and where the client has failed to accept and acknowledge a written report setting out the:

  (i) extent of the risk;
  (ii) need for the client to instruct or permit the instruction from time to time of all necessary experts including counsel;
  (iii) need for the client to provide promptly and at all times complete and accurate information and to keep the litigation department informed on a timely basis of any material changes in circumstances and to provide promptly copies of all documents served from time to time including notices, requests for information, court orders and correspondence;
  (iv) need for the client to make payment on account of all experts and counsels fees to be incurred.

(c) All cases where the request to start proceedings or lodge an appeal or undertake action is received from the client less than 14 working days before a period of limitation is due to expire.
(d) All cases where a client requests representation at a hearing less than 10 working days before its date, save a hearing purely for procedural directions where five working days shall be taken as substituted for 10 working days.
(e) Where there is evidence that past statements by the client and third parties conflict or might conflict with present instructions leading to a risk of perjured evidence being given at any hearing or in a witness statement or affidavit.
(f) Where advice being given to the client conflicts either tactically or as a matter of interpretation of law with advice previously given or now being given by an expert.
(g) Cases where the projected timescale for a hearing is likely to lead to the fee earner responsible for the case being absent from the office for a continuous period in excess of three days.
(h) Cases where a client is seeking to instruct the practice in place of a previous solicitor.
(i) Cases where a client is seeking to sue or complain about a previous solicitor or other professional.
(j) Cases where publicity is likely to ensue.

Procedures to manage cases falling outside acceptable risk levels

(a) Details of all cases likely to fall outside acceptable risk levels shall be given to [*name of person responsible/overall risk manager*] by means of a short written synopsis of the factors suggesting the case is likely to fall outside acceptable risk levels.
(b) In addition to any other risk assessment procedures specific approval to undertake the case should be sought from the department head.
(c) All cases currently assessed as falling outside acceptable risk levels, being undertaken, will be identified on the file reviews of the fee earner concerned.

(d) Similarly, details will be supplied to [*name of person responsible/overall risk manager*] in the event of any reassessment of a case resulting in an assessment that this now is likely to fall outside risk levels.

(e) Non-director fee earners to report at not more than one month intervals to the department head unless or until instructed reports at shorter or longer intervals are required by the department head or circumstances make it appropriate to report to department head earlier.

Making wills

1.   Generic risks

The main risks associated with making wills is professional negligence. Factors that may result in a claim of professional negligence include:

(a) not following clients instructions with regard to the contents of the will;
(b) not 'chasing up' client to complete the exercise when they have previously been sent a draft will;
(c) not acting upon the clients instructions within a reasonable period of time; and
(d) not checking wills executed without the supervision of the fee earner to ensure validity.

Other risks associated with will drafting are:

2.   Lack of sufficient communication

Lack of sufficient communication can lead to:

(a) prejudice to clients interests;
(b) client complaint;
(c) cost reduction in order to accommodate client concerns.

3.   Complexity of the law

(a) Availability of up-to-date resources which need to be accessed.
(b) Variety of matters within the ambit of will drafting.
(c) Assessment of relevant issues and potential problems.

4.   Administration of advice to clients

Including assessment of:

(a) the need for advice and assistance from experts such as accountants and independent financial advisers (IFAs);
(b) estimated future costs and updating thereof;
(c) quality of historic evidence (where relevant);
(d) quality of experts.

5. *Breaches of professional codes of conduct*

(a) Identifying actual or potential conflicts of interests bearing in mind that the practice may have acted for other affected parties.
(b) Supplying costs information at the outset of a transaction, particularly where the course the matter will follow is unknown at that time.
(c) Updating on costs information.
(d) Generally complying with requirements for client care.

6. *Failure to recover all or part of our fees*

(a) Requesting money on account at inception and appropriate stages in a matter, particularly where disbursements are incurred.
(b) Prompt delivery of bills of costs on an interim and final basis.
(c) Making distributions from funds held on client account without ensuring sufficient is held back to pay our fees and disbursements.

7. *Money laundering*

(a) Receipt of unusual instructions regarding the acceptance and transmission of funds.
(b) Receipt of unexpected or larger than expected sums of money on account of costs or otherwise.
(c) Receipt of cash.
(d) Failure to notify suspicions of money laundering to the MLRO.

Cases outside acceptable risk levels

(a) [*Matters outside the categories allocated to individual fee earners in the annexed allocation of will drafting*].
(b) All cases where the risk to the client of failure is known or suspected to exceed £1 million and where the client has failed to accept and acknowledge a written report setting out the need for the client to:

   (i) permit the instruction from time to time of all necessary experts including counsel.
   (ii) provide promptly and at all times complete and accurate information.
   (iii) make payment on account of all experts and counsels fees to be incurred.

(c) Where advice being given to the client conflicts with advice previously given or now being given by an expert.
(d) Cases where a client is seeking to instruct the practice in place of a previous solicitor.
(e) Cases where a client is seeking to sue or complain about a previous solicitor or other professional.
(f) Cases where publicity is likely to ensue.

Procedures to manage cases falling outside acceptable risk levels

(a) Details of all cases likely to fall outside acceptable risk levels shall be given to the overall risk manager by means of a short written synopsis of the factors suggesting the case is likely to fall outside acceptable risk levels.
(b) In addition to any other risk assessment procedures, specific approval to undertake the case should be sought from the department head.
(c) All cases currently assessed as falling outside acceptable risk levels, being undertaken, will be identified on the file reviews of the fee earner concerned.
(d) Similarly, details will be supplied to the overall risk manager in the event of any reassessment of a case resulting in an assessment that this now is likely to fall outside risk levels.
(e) Non-director fee earners to report at not more than one month intervals to the department head unless or until instructed reports at shorter or longer intervals are required by the department head or circumstances make it appropriate to report to the department head earlier.

Probate work

The main risks associated with probate work are:

1.   Professional negligence

Failure to meet time limits particularly relating to:

(a) the payment of inheritance tax on time;
(b) the submission of HM Revenue and Customs tax returns during the administration of an estate;
(c) completion of deeds of variation;
(d) submitting a claim under the Inheritance (Provision for Family and Dependants) Act 1975 within six months of the grant of probate.

2.   Delay and lack of sufficient communication

This can lead to a risk of:

(a) prejudice to clients interests;
(b) client complaint;
(c) cost reduction in order to accommodate client concerns;
(d) court judgement of maladministration.

3.   Complexity of the law

(a) Availability of up-to-date resources which need to be accessed.
(b) Variety of matters within the ambit of probate work.
(c) Assessment of relevant issues and potential problems.

4.   *Administration of advice to clients*

Including assessment of:

(a) the need for advice and assistance from experts such as accountants and IFAs;
(b) estimated future costs and updating thereof;
(c) quality of historic evidence (where relevant);
(d) quality of experts.

5.   *Breaches of professional codes of conduct*

(a) Identifying actual or potential conflicts of interests bearing in mind that the practice may have acted for other affected parties.
(b) Supplying costs information at the outset of a transaction, particularly where the course of matter will follow is unknown at that time.
(c) Updating on costs information.
(d) Generally complying with requirements for client care.

6.   *Failure to recover all or part of our fees*

(a) Requesting money on account at inception and appropriate stages in a matter, particularly where disbursements are incurred.
(b) Prompt delivery of bills of costs on an interim and final basis.
(c) Making distributions from funds held on client account without ensuring sufficient is held back to pay our fees and disbursements.

7.   *Money laundering*

(a) Receipt of unusual instructions regarding the acceptance and transmission of funds.
(b) Receipt of unexpected or larger than expected sums of money on account of costs or otherwise.
(c) Receipt of cash.
(d) Failure to notify suspicions of money laundering to the MLRO.

Cases outside acceptable risk levels

(a) [*Matters outside the categories allocated to individual fee earners in the annexed allocation of probate work*].
(b) All cases where the risk to the client of failure is known or suspected to exceed £1 million and where the client has failed to accept and acknowledge a written report setting out the extent of the need for the client:

   (i)   the need for the client to permit the instruction from time to time of all necessary experts including counsel;

(ii) the need for the client to provide promptly and at all times complete and accurate information and to keep the probate department informed on a timely basis of any material changes in circumstances and to provide promptly copies of all documents including the disclosure of all assets and liabilities and all lifetime gifts;

(iii) the need for the client to make payment on account of all experts and counsels fees to be incurred.

(f) Where advice being given to the client conflicts with advice previously given or now being given by an expert.

(g) Cases where a client is seeking to instruct the practice in place of a previous solicitor.

(h) Cases where a client is seeking to sue or complain about a previous solicitor or other professional.

(i) Cases where publicity is likely to ensue.

Procedures to manage cases falling outside acceptable risk levels

(a) Details of all cases likely to fall outside acceptable risk levels shall be given to the overall risk manager by means of a short written synopsis of the factors suggesting the case is likely to fall outside acceptable risk levels.

(b) In addition to any other risk assessment procedures, specific approval to undertake the case should be sought from the department head.

(c) All cases currently assessed as falling outside acceptable risk levels, being undertaken, will be identified on the file reviews of the fee earner concerned.

(d) Similarly, details will be supplied to the overall risk manager in the event of any reassessment of a case resulting in an assessment that this now is likely to fall outside risk levels.

(e) Non-director fee earner to report at not more than one month intervals to the department head unless or until instructed reports at shorter or longer intervals are required by the department head or circumstances make it appropriate to report to the department head earlier.

Family work

The main risks associated with family work are:

1. *Professional negligence*

(a) Failure to meet time limits, particularly relating to:

- protocol requirements;
- starting of proceedings and giving of notices;
- dealing with procedural directions;
- hearing dates;
- appeals.

(b) Delay and lack of sufficient communication leading to risk of:

- prejudice to client's case;
- client complaint;
- costs reduction on assessment or by need to accommodate client concerns;
- adverse procedural orders.

(c) Complexity of the law.

- Availability of up-to-date resources which need to be accessed.
- Variety of matters within the ambit of family work.
- Assessment of potential outcomes and chances of success.

(d) Administration of advice to client including assessment of:

- the need for advice and assistance from experts and counsel;
- alternative funding arrangements;
- cost/benefit to client;
- estimated future costs and updating thereof;
- quality of historic evidence (where relevant);
- quality of consultants and of evidence;
- probability of success;
- possibility of costs being awarded against client;
- desirability of alternative dispute resolution procedures.

2. *Breaches of professional codes of conduct*

(a) Identifying actual or potential conflicts of interests bearing in mind that the practice may have acted for other affected parties.
(b) Supplying sufficient costs information at the outset of a transaction, particularly where the course the matter will follow is unknown at that time.
(c) Updating on costs information.
(d) Generally complying with requirements for client care.

3. *Failure to recover all or part of our fees*

(a) Requesting money on account at inception and appropriate stages in a matter, particularly where disbursements are incurred.
(b) Prompt delivery of bills of costs on an interim and final basis.
(c) Explanation of the limitations on costs recovery from opposing party.

4. *Money laundering*

(a) Receipt of unusual instructions regarding the acceptance and transmission of funds.
(b) Receipt of unexpected or larger than expected sums of money on account of costs or otherwise.
(c) Receipt of cash.
(d) Failure to notify suspicions of money laundering to the MLRO.

Cases outside acceptable risk levels

(a) [*Matters outside the categories allocated to individual fee earners in the annexed allocation of family work*].
(b) All cases where the risk to the client of failure is known or suspected to exceed £1 million and where the client has failed to accept and acknowledge a written report setting out the extent of the need for the client to:

  (i) permit the instruction from time to time of all necessary experts including counsel;
  (ii) provide promptly and at all times complete and accurate information and to keep the family department informed on a timely basis of any material changes in circumstances and to provide promptly copies of all documents served from time to time including notices, requests for information, court orders and correspondence;
  (iii) make payment on account of all experts and counsels fees to be incurred.

(c) All cases where the request to start proceedings or lodge an appeal or undertake action is received from the client less than 14 working days before a period of limitation is due to expire.
(d) All cases where a client requests representation at a hearing less than 10 working days before its date, save a hearing purely for procedural directions where five working days shall be taken as substituted for 10 working days.
(e) Where there is evidence that past statements by the client and third parties conflict or might conflict with present instructions leading to a risk of perjured evidence being given at any hearing or in a witness statement or affidavit.
(f) Where advice being given to the client conflicts either tactically or as a matter of interpretation of law with advice previously given or now being given by an expert.
(g) Cases where the projected timescale for a hearing is likely to lead to the fee earner responsible for the case being absent from the office for a continuous period in excess of three days.
(h) Cases where a client is seeking to instruct the practice in place of a previous solicitor.
(i) Cases where a client is seeking to sue or complain about a previous solicitor or other professional.
(j) Cases where publicity is likely to ensue.

Procedures to manage cases falling outside acceptable risk levels

(a) Details of all cases likely to fall outside acceptable risk levels shall be given to the overall risk manager by means of a short written synopsis of the factors suggesting the case is likely to fall outside acceptable risk levels.
(b) In addition to any other risk assessment procedures specific approval to undertake the case should be sought from the department head.
(c) All cases currently assessed as falling outside acceptable risk levels, being undertaken, will be identified on the file reviews of the fee earner concerned.
(d) Similarly, details will be supplied to the overall risk manager in the event of any reassessment of a case resulting in an assessment that this now is likely to fall outside risk levels.

(e) Non-director fee earners to report at not more than one month intervals to the department head unless or until instructed reports at shorter or longer intervals are required by the department head or circumstances make it appropriate to report to department head earlier.

Annex 6D
Generic risk table

Area of law	Generic risk	Preventive/ mitigatory actions
Private client		
Wills	1. Does the client have capacity? Is a doctor's report required? 2. Who is my client? Take instructions from the client. 3. Does the client require tax planning advice? If so, advise on both inheritance tax (IHT) and capital gains tax (CGT). 4. Has the client approved the draft? Do not let too much time elapse after draft sent out. 5. Is the client in danger of dying before being able to sign? 6. Is the client signing not under our supervision? Send appropriate instruction sheet. 7. Is this a case where there is a potential Inheritance Act claim? 8. Has appropriate terms letter been sent?	
Estates	1. Where is the will? Is this the last will? Is there a codicil? 2. Is the estate taxable? 3. Are you sure you have details of all assets? 4. On an intestacy are you sure you have details of all relatives and have an up-to-date family tree? 5. Is any property insured? 6. Advertise for creditors. 7. Have you written to all beneficiaries? 8. Is an interim distribution appropriate? If so, have you carefully calculated and made allowances for all outstanding debts and professional charges? 9. Is a deed of variation required? 10. Has a professional valuation of items in the estate been obtained? 11. Has the appropriate terms letter been sent?	
Trusts	1. Regularly review investment policy. 2. Observe deadline dates for tax returns. 3. Are regular income payments appropriate? 4. Has appropriate terms letter been sent? Remember, terms letter on previous probate matter is not sufficient for the resulting trust matter.	

Area of law	Generic risk	Preventive/ mitigatory actions
Powers of attorney	1. Does the client have sufficient capacity? Is a doctor's report required? 2. Remember who is your client; the donor, not the attorney/s. 3. Remember to observe time limits when registering the power of attorney.	
General advice when dealing with the elderly	1. Remember who is your client. 2. Does the client have capacity? Is a doctor's report required? 3. Has appropriate terms letter been sent? 4. When dealing with clients who wish to gift their property, make sure you fully advise them of the implications with regard to tax, bankruptcy or divorce of donee, nursing home fees and assistance from the local authority, etc. 5. Does the client require investment advice?	
Domestic sale	1. Missed key dates. 2. Advice – effects on property now and in the future. 3. Documentation/procedure – effect on future property rights and value.	
Domestic purchase	1. Missed key dates. 2. Advice – effects on property now and in the future. 3. Documentation/procedure – effect on future property rights and value.	
Re-mortgages	1. Missed key dates. 2. Advice – effects on property now and in the future. 3. Documentation/procedure – effect on future property rights and value.	
Other property transactions	1. Missed key dates. 2. Advice – effects on property now and in the future. 3. Documentation/procedure – effect on future property rights and value.	
Company commercial		
Business start-ups	Making sure client chooses appropriate vehicle through which to trade. (N.B. liaise with accountant/tax advisor.)	
Partnership/ shareholder agreements/company formation	1. Awareness of relevant statutory provisions/ scope for adapting these where this is permitted. 2. Arrangements with fellow partners/ shareholders, especially re: finance, management and exit.	

Area of law	Generic risk	Preventive/ mitigatory actions
Terms of business	Awareness of relevant statutory provisions/case law, especially if client deals with consumers/seeks to limit/exclude liability.	
Contracts of employment/ service agreements/ consultancy agreements	1. Is client employed/self-employed? 2. Awareness of relevant statutory provisions/case law.	
Other commercial contracts	Awareness of relevant statutory provisions depending on type of contract, especially UK and EC competition law where appropriate.	
Buying and selling businesses/companies	1. Acting for buyer – advising on pre-contract enquiries/due diligence, structure for paying consideration, transfer of key contracts, warranties/indemnities in purchase agreement and, if buying a business, TUPE implications (under Transfer of Undertakings (Protection of Employment) Regulations 2006). 2. Acting for seller – advising on seller's pre-contract enquiries and transfer of key contracts, exposure to warranties/indemnities in purchase agreement, structure for receiving consideration and, if selling a business, TUPE implications. 3. N.B. no advice given on tax issues – refer to accountant or other tax advisor.	
Intellectual property	1. Ways of protecting clients' intellectual property. Advising on procedures to be followed if registration to be involved. 2. N.B. refer client to specialist if necessary, e.g. patent agents.	
Insolvency/business breakdown	1. Awareness of relevant statutory provisions, especially during period leading up to insolvency. 2. Advice on procedure/matters to be dealt with.	
Commercial property		
Sale of freehold	Title and replies to enquiries.	
Purchase of freehold	Investigation of title, searches and enquiries.	
Grant of lease	Drafting and advice to the landlord.	
Taking a lease	Approving draft and advice to tenant.	
Landlord and Tenant Act 1954, s.25 notices to quit	Notices and time limits.	
Planning law	Interpretation of consents and refusals. Time limits for appeals.	

Area of law	Generic risk	Preventive/ mitigatory actions
Liquor licensing	Notices and time limits.	
Internal appeals procedures	1. Missed deadlines to appeal on employee's decision. 2. Use internal procedures before issue court/ tribunal proceedings. 3. Proportionality.	
Tribunal proceedings	1. Missed key dates. 2. Time limits for issuing claims. 3. Time limits for filing respondent's defence. 4. Time limits for exchanging bundles. 5. Time limits for exchanging statements. 6. Hearing dates.	
County court proceedings	1. Missed key dates. 2. Issuing proceedings. 3. Filing defences. 4. Exchanging documents. 5. Filing statements. 6. Complying with directions. 7. Hearing dates.	
Employment Appeal Tribunals	1. Missed key dates. 2. Filing notice of appeal. 3. Submitting skeleton arguments. 4. Hearing dates.	
Litigation		
Personal injury and medical negligence	1. Missed key dates, i.e. limitation period, court dates, filing documents. 2. Proportionality. 3. Advice, keep receipts for special damages. 4. Advice on contributory negligence. 5. Advice on funding, i.e. conditional fee agreement (CFA) details. 6. Are experts on third party register?	
Housing	1. Missed key dates, i.e. when notice requiring possession expires, hearing date. 2. Do they need benefit advice? 3. Proportionality on repairs.	

Debt	1. If county court proceedings:
	   • missed date for defence;
	   • filing of evidence; or
	   • court hearing.
	2. Overall view of case and best economic advice – settlement advice.
	3. Proportionality.
	4. Long-term effect on credit rating.
	5. Advice on limitation period.	

Area of law	Generic risk	Preventive/ mitigatory actions
Consumer	1. Advice on law and progression of matter to court. 2. Costs involved. 3. Proportionality. 4. The use and cost of experts and third party register. 5. Practical solutions, use of: (i) Trading standards office; (ii) Independent ombudsman.	
Family		
Private law children	Missed key dates, i.e. court dates, filing statements.	
Public law children	Missed key dates, i.e. court dates, filing statements.	
Divorce	1. Missed key dates. 2. Advice – effects on property and making a will.	
Ancillary relief	1. Missed key dates. 2. Advice – effects on property and making a will. 3. Proportionality.	
Domestic violence	Missed key dates.	
Co-habitee disputes	1. Missed key dates. 2. Advice – wills and property.	

Annex 6E

Conflicts of interests policy

Policy statement

[The practice recognises that conflicts of interests constitute risks to the practice, and that unless handled properly and in accordance with regulatory requirements, can lead to complaints and claims against the practice. They can not only lead to serious financial consequences for the practice, but also severely damage its reputation. [*Name*] is responsible for the conflicts of interests policy.

It has therefore been decided that, on every occasion that a conflict of interest is identified, the practice will decline instructions and refer actual or potential clients to other practices in accordance with the referral policy.]

[*OR*]

[In order to ensure that the risks associated with conflicts of interests are managed, the practice will ensure that the positive outcomes-focused regulation (OFR) mandatory outcomes and indicative behaviours as indicated below, will at all times be satisfied, and the negative mandatory outcomes and indicative behaviours, also listed below, will be avoided. To that end, the procedures in this policy have been developed, and they will be strictly observed. Any breach of these procedures will be treated seriously, and could result in disciplinary proceedings.]

Scope

This policy applies to all individuals working at every level and grade, including partners, senior managers, officers, directors, employees, consultants, contractors, trainees, home workers, part-time and fixed-term employees, casual and agency staff and volunteers, collectively referred to as staff in this policy.

Application of the policy

The general rule is that the practice must not act if:

(a) there is a conflict of interests;
(b) there is a significant risk of a conflict; or
(c) the practice holds material confidential information for a past or present client, and that confidentiality would be put at risk by the practice acting.

Without exception, when a new matter is begun, the fee earner will ensure that a conflict of interest check is undertaken on the client and any other party that is involved in the matter. This check is completed by: [*name*].

[*Indicate exactly how the checks will be undertaken.*

Points to consider.

- *Checking the practice's database of clients and opponents by name and address.*
- *Sending 'round robin' emails or other communications to all fee earners within the practice to see if anyone is aware of any actual or potential conflict of interest, or breach of confidentiality. Under normal circumstances, this measure alone may not be sufficient.]*

There are occasions when all parties to a matter are not known at the beginning, in which case fee earners must remain alert to the requirement that, whenever another party joins a matter at any stage, a conflict of interest check must be undertaken on that party.

Confirmation of the completion of the conflict of interest check will be confirmed by recording the fact on [*indicate how and where the conflict check and outcome will be recorded on the matter file, e.g. on the file summary sheet (if such a document is used)*].

Conflict definitions by work type

The practice has identified the various types of conflict of interest that can occur within the range of matters that it undertakes. The list of work types is located [*insert location*].

When a conflict of interests occurs

If, on completion of a conflict of interest check, a fee earner either:

(a) has identified an actual or potential conflict of interest; or
(b) is uncertain about the result;

they must consult [*name*], whose advice will be strictly followed. The person who makes the ultimate decisions relating to conflicts of interests is the compliance officer for legal practice (COLP).

Recording

The COLP will maintain a register of conflicts of interests that have been identified.

Confidentiality

Although this policy deals with conflicts of interests, fee earners must also be aware of any matters which put at risk confidential information relating to past or present clients. If a fee earner believes that they have identified such a situation, then they must take the same action as when a conflict of interests is discovered.

Training

The practice recognises the importance of training for people who conduct conflicts of interests checks, and to this end it has been determined that training will be provided for all relevant individuals as follows:

(a) all new partners, fee earners and support staff, including secretaries, will receive training on this subject and policy as part of their initial induction;

(b) when a new partner, fee earner, and any other person likely to be involved in undertaking conflicts of interests checks joins a department or team, they will be trained on the types of conflict that apply to that department or team;

(c) everyone will receive refresher training on this subject at least [*frequency*], as part of the practice's approach to 'generic' training (see the learning and development plan).

In addition to formal training, partners and fee earners are reminded of their responsibility to ensure full compliance with the SRA Handbook, and it is therefore suggested that they refresh their memories at least annually on the part of the Handbook which deals with conflicts of interest and confidentiality (SRA Code of Conduct 2011, chapters 3 and 4).

Review

This policy will be reviewed at least annually by [*name*], and any issues that arise from the review will be reported to [*name*].

Annex 6F

Policy on financial crime

It is unfortunate that, in the eyes of criminal elements, practices are potentially 'soft targets' to be enmeshed in activities that fall under the general heading of financial crime. The practice recognises this risk and associated consequences, and has developed three policies and associated procedures intended to prevent involvement in:

- money laundering;
- mortgage fraud; and
- unlawful activities described within the Bribery Act 2010.

Combined, these policies and procedures constitute the practice's approaches and systems to combat any attempts to involve it in any aspect of financial crime.

Scope

These policies and procedures apply to all individuals working at every level and grade, including partners, senior managers, officers, directors, employees, consultants, contractors, trainees, home workers, part-time and fixed-term employees, casual and agency staff and volunteers, collectively referred to as staff in this policy.

The procedures

Anti-money laundering

The procedures relating to anti-money laundering (AML) are found in [*exact location where practice's AML policy is located*].

The person responsible for the implementation and monitoring of the AML policy is [*name*], and [he/she] will review the policy at least annually, and report the outcomes of the review to [*name*].

Prevention of mortgage fraud

The procedures relating to avoiding involvement in mortgage fraud are found in [*exact location where the practice's anti-mortgage fraud procedures are located*].

The person responsible for the implementation and monitoring of the procedures is [*name*], and [he/she] will review the policy at least annually, and report the outcomes of the review to [*name*].

Bribery Act 2010

The procedures relating to the Bribery Act 2010 are found in [*insert the exact location where the practice's Bribery Act policy is located*].

The person responsible for the implementation and monitoring of the procedures is [*name*], and [he/she] will review the policy at least annually, and report the outcomes of the review to [*name*].

Annex 6G
Anti-bribery and corruption policy

Policy statement

Offences relating to bribery and corruption carry substantial terms of imprisonment for individuals and unlimited fines for organisations. In addition, organisations that are convicted of such offences could be excluded from tendering for public contracts and face damage to their reputations.

It is the policy of the practice to conduct all business in an honest and ethical manner. The practice has a zero-tolerance approach to bribery and corruption and will take all possible measures to ensure that every aspect of its business and associated relationships is undertaken and conducted professionally, and with integrity.

The development, monitoring and management of this policy is the responsibility of [name].

Scope

This policy applies to all individuals working at all levels and grades, including partners, employees (whether permanent, fixed-term or temporary), consultants, contractors, trainees, seconded staff, home workers, casual workers and agency staff, volunteers, interns, agents, sponsors, or any other person associated with us, or any of our subsidiaries or their employees, wherever located, collectively referred to as staff in this policy.

Preventative procedures

Contracts with agents and other providers of services, and all individuals and organisations with whom the practice has a business relationship, should be considered in light of this policy and its procedures. If appropriate, consideration must be given to whether such individuals or organisations have anti-bribery and corruption policies and whether they should be made aware of the existence of the practice's policy.

Where anyone is unsure of the appropriate course of action, they must confer with [name].

Consideration must always be given to the balance between any payment made in respect of services provided, and the measurable benefit of those services.

A non-exhaustive list of the matters which must be considered in this respect is:

- what services are being provided?
- is it transparent from invoices received (where appropriate) what those services are?
- is the charge being made for the services reasonable and appropriate for the services provided?

The extent to which such consideration must be given depends on the nature of the relationship with the agent, provider of services, or other party with whom the practice has a business relationship, and the risk of bribery occurring.

Any concern about a relationship the practice has, or is about to enter into, with a provider of services, or with another individual or organisation, must be discussed with [name].

Gifts and hospitality

The provision of gifts and hospitality that are reasonable and proportionate, with regard to the relationship the practice has with an individual or organisation to whom this is offered, is not prohibited by the Bribery Act 2010.

The practice will provide such gifts and hospitality as the partners consider appropriate, but not in circumstances where this might influence, or reasonably be perceived to influence, the improper performance of a relevant function.

A non-exhaustive list of the types of gifts and entertainment which the practice will provide includes:

- seasonal gifts as a reflection of good relationships;
- promotional items bearing the practice's name;
- lunches;
- tickets to events.

The practice's policy is that all offers to provide gifts or hospitality must be authorised by a partner, prior to them being made to a third party. All gifts shall be given openly, not secretly.

On some occasions, offers of gifts and hospitality are received. The practice's policy is that such offers should not be accepted without the approval of a partner. In deciding whether to give such approval, the partner will consider the practice's relationship with the individual or organisation making the offer, and he/she will remain mindful of the practice's duty to act in the best interests of its clients at all times. If there is any doubt or concern about the propriety of receiving any gifts and/or hospitality, [name] must be consulted.

To assist in monitoring compliance with, and reviewing the effectiveness of, this policy, a record of all gifts and hospitality provided to and from the practice, and of those offered to, and accepted by, the practice, is kept by [name], and staff and partners should ensure that [he/she] is advised of all offers and acceptances accordingly.

Charitable donations

The practice makes financial donations to various charities, and may occasionally provide pro bono services to clients who are considered to be appropriate recipients of such donations and services. When doing so, a non-exhaustive list of checks which should be considered is:

(a) identifying whether the charity is registered;
(b) ensuring that money is donated to the organisation directly, and not to an individual, should there be any doubt about the links that that individual has with the organisation;
(c) exercising caution when making a donation if the charity has a connection to a client or an organisation which may influence the practice's business.

To assist in monitoring compliance with, and reviewing the effectiveness of, this policy, a record of all donations made, and pro bono services provided to, charitable and other similar organisations, is kept by [name], and staff and partners should ensure that [he/she] is advised of such donations and services that have been provided.

Enforcement and breach

Any breach of the policy is a risk to the practice and is, accordingly, likely to be regarded as a serious disciplinary offence. When, at any time, a breach of the policy been identified, an investigation will be undertaken by [name] in order to ascertain the full facts and circumstances of the breach. At the same time, the policy will be reviewed by [name], and any modification to the policy, or other appropriate remedial action that is identified, will be immediately actioned.

All partners and staff are under a duty to immediately report an actual, suspected or attempted breach of the policy caused by a third party to [name].

Training

The practice will provide training on this subject at least biennially for everyone, or more frequently if deemed necessary.

Monitoring and review

[Name] will monitor the operation of this policy, and will conduct a review at least annually, following which [he/she] will submit a report to [name].

7 Client care

Practices should note that the client care manager should be someone with appropriate seniority to take on such a role.

For a client care policy, see **Annex 7A**.

For a client facing complaints handling procedure, see **Annex 7B**.

For a complaints procedure, see **Annex 7C**.

Annex 7A
Client care policy

The person with overall responsibility for the client care policy is [*name*].

[*Name of practice*] is committed to delivering excellent client service and client care. Our client care policy describes what this commitment means in practice and what our clients can expect from us. We will endeavour to adhere to the principle of putting our clients first, thereby ensuring that service excellence is an integral part of the planning and delivery of all services to our clients.

In order to achieve client service excellence, [*name of practice*] aims at all times to:

- provide clients with a high quality, professional and consistent service;
- act in accordance with the SRA Code of Conduct 2011 and other relevant regulatory requirements;
- act in a respectful and courteous manner in all dealings with clients;
- represent our clients' best interests;
- ensure all our staff fully understand and are committed to client care in all their interactions with clients;
- ensure we communicate effectively with our clients and with an agreed mode of communication upon request; and
- give clear legal advice.

At [*name of practice*], we make sure that our clients receive a client care letter that fully explains the level of service they will receive. In addition, we will name the person responsible for individual matters, his or her position in the practice and his or her qualifications. The client care letter will give the name of the supervisor responsible for each matter, and the name of the person who is responsible for dealing with any complaints.

In order that we can continually improve our service, we actively encourage and value feedback from our clients. We will use various methods to elicit feedback, including client satisfaction surveys and post-matter questionnaires. In addition, we monitor and evaluate client complaints to identify and address shortcomings and failings in our standard of service. Such feedback is essential to help continually gauge client perceptions of our service.

[*Name of practice*] has the above measures in place to ensure we achieve our goal of providing a quality service.

This policy will be reviewed annually on [*date*] by [*name of member in senior management team*] as part of the annual review of client care and as part of the annual review of risk, both of which are in line with Lexcel requirements.

Annex 7B
Complaints handling procedure (client version)

Our complaints policy

We are committed to providing a high quality legal service to all our clients. When something goes wrong, we need you to tell us about it. This will help us to improve our standards.

Our complaints procedure

If you have a complaint about our service or a bill that we have rendered on or both, please contact us with the details.

The person to contact is [name], and [he/she] can be reached at:

[*Full postal address, direct line telephone number and email address*]

What will happen next?

1. We will send you a letter acknowledging receipt of your complaint within [*insert a realistic number*] days of us receiving the complaint, enclosing a copy of this procedure.
2. We will then investigate your complaint. This will normally involve passing your complaint to [name] who will review your file and speak to the member of staff who acted for you.
3. [Name] will then invite you to a meeting to discuss and hopefully resolve your complaint. This will be done within [*insert a realistic number*] days of sending you the acknowledgement letter.
4. Within [*insert a realistic number*] days of the meeting, [name] will write to you to confirm what took place and any solutions [he/she] has agreed with you.
5. If you do not want a meeting or it is not possible, [name] will send you a detailed written reply to your complaint, including [his/her] suggestions for resolving the matter, within [*insert a realistic number*] days of sending you the acknowledgement letter.
6. At this stage, if you are still not satisfied, you should contact us again and we will arrange for [*another partner or someone unconnected with the matter at the practice to review the decision, or, for a sole practitioner: [name] to review [his/her] own decision or insert appropriate alternative, such as review by another local solicitor or mediation*].
7. We will write to you within [*insert a realistic number*] days of receiving your request for a review, confirming our final position on your complaint and explaining our reasons.
8. If we have to change any of the timescales above, we will let you know and explain why.

9. If you are still not satisfied, you can then contact the Legal Ombudsman at:

PO Box 6806
Wolverhampton
WV1 9WJ
Tel: 0300 555 0333 or 0121 245 3050
Email: enquiries@legalombudsman.org.uk

There are time limits within which complaints must be made to the Legal Ombudsman, as indicated below.

Generally speaking, your complaint should be made to the Ombudsman no later than 12 months from when the problem occurred or from when you should reasonably have become aware of the problem.

Additionally, you should make your complaint to the Ombudsman within six months of receiving a final response from us following the complaint that you have made to us.

Normally, your complaint needs to fall inside both rules if the Ombudsman is going to investigate it.

You also need to be aware that the Ombudsman only deals with complaints from the following:

(a) an enterprise which, at the time that the complaint is made, is a micro-enterprise within the meaning of arts.1, 2(1) and (3) of the Annex to Commission Recommendation 2003/361/EC, as that Recommendation had effect at the date it was adopted;
(b) a charity with an annual income net of tax of less than £1 million at the time at which the complainant refers the complaint to the respondent;
(c) a club, association or organisation, the affairs of which are managed by its members or a committee or committees of its members, with an annual income net of tax of less than £1 million at the time at which the complainant refers the complaint to the respondent;
(d) a trustee of a trust with an asset value of less than £1 million at the time at which the complainant refers the complaint to the respondent;
(e) a personal representative of an estate of a person; or
(f) a beneficiary of an estate of a person.

Annex 7C
Complaints procedure

General

[*Name*] is responsible for developing, monitoring, assessing and managing the complaints procedure.

Definition

The practice has adopted and adapted the Legal Ombudsman's definition of a complaint, being:

an expression of dissatisfaction with a service relating to an act or omission about a service provided to:

- a complainant (including the client);
- another authorised person who procured the service on behalf of the complainant; or
- a personal representative/trustee where the complainant is a beneficiary of the trust/ estate;

which cannot be immediately resolved to the complainant's satisfaction by the fee earner and the matter supervisor.

Implementation

At the outset of every matter clients will be informed:

(a) of their right to complain about either the service they have received, or a bill that has been rendered, or both;
(b) to whom they should complain;
(c) that the practice has a complaints procedure, a copy of which will be supplied to them upon their request, and in any case if they make a complaint.

When a complaint has been made, the recipients of a complaint will immediately inform their supervisor, or if they are self supervising, they will inform [*name*].

Immediately upon receipt of the complaint, complainants will be informed in writing:

(a) how and by whom their complaint will be handled; and
(b) when they can expect either an initial or substantive response to their complaint.

This information is contained in the procedure document that is sent to the complainant.

The complaint will be recorded and held centrally by [*name*].

[*Name*] will adhere to the procedure contained in the complaints document that is sent to the complainant. This is to ensure that:

(a) the complaint will be thoroughly investigated, using whatever means and enquiries [*name*] considers to be appropriate, with whomever [*name*] considers appropriate;
(b) the cause of the complaint is identified; any appropriate redress is offered to the client; and
(c) any process or procedure which, it is felt, contributed to the complaint and needs to be revised or amended in any way, will be amended as required.

Responsibility and reviews

[*Name*] will conduct the following reviews at least annually:

(a) A review of the complaints procedures, including that which is sent to clients, to ensure that they are being used effectively throughout the practice, following which any necessary amendments will be made.
(b) A review of all of the claims and complaints that have been received by the practice within the previous 12 months in order to:

  (i)   identify any causation trends;
  (ii) make corrections to any processes or procedures that are considered necessary to assist in the prevention of future trend occurrences; and
  (iii) compile a report from the findings, to be submitted to the [risk manager/ partnership/executive/management board/*other*].

8 File and case management

For a client instruction procedure, see **Annex 8A**.

For an external service provider evaluation template, see **Annex 8B**.

For a procedure for the use of external service providers, see **Annex 8C**.

For a file closure form, see **Annex 8D**.

Annex 8A
Client instruction procedure

Introduction

[Name] is responsible for the client instruction procedures. These procedures must be read in conjunction with the client care and conflicts of interests policies. It is the policy of the practice that decisions regarding the acceptance, declining or ceasing of instructions will be made in a manner which complies with:

- all regulatory requirements;
- the practice's equality and diversity policy; and
- the general principles listed below.

Scope

These procedures apply to all individuals with fee earning responsibilities that include the acceptance, rejection and termination of instructions from clients.

Purpose of the procedures

The procedures are intended to ensure a common approach to the accepting, declining and ceasing of instructions, as part of the practice's risk management framework.

These procedures deal with:

- the handling of enquiries, and the receipt of instructions, from existing and new clients;
- the acceptance of instructions;
- decisions to decline instructions; and
- ceasing to act for clients.

Any alterations to, or variations from, these procedures can only be made with the permission of [name], and they will be documented within the procedures.

Prohibited circumstances

When any decisions are being made to accept, decline, or terminate instructions, the decision maker will ensure that the circumstances described below will not apply following his or her decisions. If there is the slightest doubt or suspicion that any of them may apply either before or following the acceptance of instructions, guidance must be sought from [name].

- Acting for a client when instructions are given by someone else, or by only one client when you act jointly for others, unless you are satisfied that the person providing the instructions has the authority to do so on behalf of all of the clients.

- Ceasing to act for a client without good reason and without providing reasonable notice.
- Entering into unlawful fee arrangements such as an unlawful contingency fee.
- Acting for a client when there are reasonable grounds for believing that the instructions are affected by duress or undue influence, without satisfying yourself that they represent the client's wishes.

Receiving enquiries

Enquiries relating to actual or potential instructions are received from a number of sources including:

- enquiries in person to an office;
- correspondence to the practice generally;
- correspondence to a fee earner individually;
- telephone calls to the practice's switchboard;
- telephone calls to a fee earner individually;
- email to the practice's 'enquiries' email address;
- email to a fee earner individually;
- to the practice's central fax machine; or
- to a departmental fax machine.

Personal enquiries at an office

When an enquiry is made in person at reception, [*fully describe the steps that must be taken in dealing with such enquiries*].

[*Points to consider:*

- *Who should the receptionist contact?*
- *What happens if a suitable fee earner is not available?*
- *The practice will probably want to emphasise that no enquirer must leave the building 'empty handed'.*]

Enquiries by correspondence or fax

If an enquiry for a potential instruction is received by post or fax, [*indicate exactly the steps to be taken when dealing with such enquiries*].

[*Points to consider:*

- *What happens if it is addressed to a fee earner; particularly if it is not the type of matter that that fee earner would deal with?*
- *Should all enquiries automatically be forwarded to a partner/supervisor/team leader for a decision to accept and allocate?*]

Enquiries by email

[*Fully describe the steps that must be taken to deal with such enquiries.*

Points to consider:

- *What should be done if it is received direct by a fee earner?*
- *Should all such enquiries be sent to a partner/supervisor/team leader?*]

Enquiries by telephone

When an enquiry is received by the switchboard, [*fully describe the steps that must be taken to deal with such enquiries*].

[*Points to consider.*

- *What should be done if it is received direct by a fee earner?*
- *What should be done if that fee earner is not an appropriate person to deal with the potential matter?*
- *Should all such enquiries be sent to a partner/supervisor/team leader?*]

Accepting and declining instructions

The way that a decision is made to accept or decline instructions will depend on whether the instructions are:

(a) from an existing client;
(b) of a type similar to those previously received from a client;
(c) from a new client;
(d) within the competence of the practice to undertake. When any instructions or potential instructions are received by the practice, the person making the decision to accept or decline must always consider whether or not the practice has the necessary knowledge and experience amongst its fee earners to undertake the instructions;
(e) of a risk level that is acceptable to the practice;
(f) within the capacity of the practice to undertake them. When any instructions or potential instructions are received by the practice, the person making the decision to accept or decline must always take into account whether or not the practice has sufficient fee earner capacity to undertake the instructions.

The following procedures will be followed when instructions from new or existing clients are received.

From an existing client

[*Describe exactly how the decision will be made to accept or decline instructions, and by whom.*

Points to consider:

- *Are these instructions consistent with others that have been received from the client?*
- *If not, what different considerations will be needed in making the decision whether to accept or decline?*
- *What effect will a higher than normal risk level have on whether to accept or decline?*]

From a new client

[*Describe exactly how the decision will be made to accept or decline instructions, and by whom.*]

Declining instructions

If a decision is made to decline instructions, the client/potential client will be informed in writing.

If the reason for declining the instructions is one of competence or capacity on the part of the practice, consideration will be given to assisting the enquirer to find a practice that could deal with the matter. If the declining is for any other reason, this assistance will not be provided.

Where it has been decided to assist the enquirer to find an appropriate service provider, under normal circumstances the practice will recommend at least two or three providers from which the enquirer can make the final choice. This is to safeguard the practice's interests should another provider not meet the enquirer's expectations. As an alternative, the enquirer could be signposted to the local Law Society who may be able to assist.

Ceasing to act

Where a fee earner is of the opinion that the practice should terminate instructions, he/she must discuss the issue with his/her supervisor, or if a supervisor is not readily available, with [*name*]. If the fee earner is a partner or supervisor, he/she must consult [*name*].

If a decision is made to terminate instructions, the client will be informed in writing, together with the reason for the decision.

Training

Training in these procedures will be provided as part of the inductions for all new appointees, including partners, fee earners and support staff and, if considered appropriate, follow-up training will be given as part of the generic training programme that the practice has in place. This will be reflected in the annual practice wide training plan.

Review

These procedures will be reviewed at least annually by [*name*], and any amendments that are made will be notified to all members of the practice.

Annex 8B
External service provider evaluation template

Name of provider	Chambers/Practice/Organisation	
Date of evaluation	**Matter number**	**Client name**

Performance evaluation

[Insert (✓) in the appropriate column. Additional notes are not mandatory unless the evaluator considers it necessary]

Criteria	At standard	Not at standard	Notes
Interpersonal & communication skills with clients	☐	☐	
Speed of response	☐	☐	
Thoroughness & quality of reports	☐	☐	
Costs	☐	☐	
Specialist expertise	☐	☐	
Length of experience	☐	☐	

Other criteria used *[Please specify and evaluate]*

Criteria	At standard	Not at standard	Notes
	☐	☐	
	☐	☐	

Overall evaluation category

[Tick the appropriate category]

A ☐   B ☐   C ☐

If category 'C', indicate the name of the individual with specific details:

Evaluation category confirmation	
Name of person authorising	
Signature	
Date	
Any other relevant information	

Annex 8C
Procedure for the use of external service providers

Introduction

From time to time, it is necessary for the practice to consult with, and employ, counsel, independent experts, and other service providers. [*Name*] is responsible for the management of this procedure.

Scope

These procedures apply to all individuals with fee earning responsibilities.

Selection criteria

Although the circumstances of an individual matter may require specific skills and qualities from an external service provider, the following criteria will form the basis of most instructions to such people (the list is not exhaustive):

(a) interpersonal and communication skills with clients;
(b) speed of response;
(c) thoroughness and quality of reports;
(d) costs;
(e) specialist expertise;
(f) length of experience.

The practice maintains a record of approved external service providers whose work does not fall under the auspices of outsourcing, and this is retained [*insert where the record(s) are kept*], and under normal circumstances a service provider will be chosen from this list. In circumstances where an approved provider is not available, fee earners may appoint an alternative, but only after consultation with [*name*].

In circumstances where a 'new', previously unused service provider is instructed, their performance must be closely monitored against the practice's selection criteria (see earlier) during the provision of the service, and a full record, including an evaluation of performance, will be kept and forwarded to [*name of person who retains the central records*] for retention.

If the performance of the previously unused service provider is satisfactory, then consideration will be given to their being placed on the approved list. [*If the practice uses the A, B, C categories of evaluation, then an additional sentence can be added to say that the previously unused service provider will be graded as either an A, B, or C category.*] Their inclusion will normally be approved by [*name*].

Consultation with the client

Whenever possible, clients will be consulted when the selection of a service provider is made. If a client chooses an expert about whom the practice has reservations, the fee earner will discuss the choice with the client in the light of those reservations, but the client has the right to override such reservations, subject to normal professional standards on the propriety of all actions taken for clients.

If a client makes a selection based on criteria that would contravene the practice's equality and diversity policy, or would put the practice at risk of breaching any legislative or regulatory obligations, this will be explained to the client, and if the client insists on such an appointment, there will be consultation with [name], with the likely outcome that the practice would cease acting in the matter.

When a selection has been made, the client will be informed:

(a) of the name and status of the service provider;
(b) how long they are likely to take in providing the service;
(c) the likely fees and disbursements of the provider (if the client will be expected to meet these).

Briefing service providers

Service providers will normally receive instructions through any of the following: letter, formal written brief, telephone conversation, or at a meeting. Those instructions must be thorough and clear.

Where instructions are provided orally, they will be subsequently confirmed in writing.

Where appropriate, experts should be made aware of the rules of court and any court orders with which they will be required to comply. In all cases, a note of the instructions, or a copy of them, must be retained on the matter file.

Receipt of advice/reports from service providers

On receipt of advice from any service provider, the fee earner must consider its suitability and value. If the advice or its presentation is considered inappropriate, or for whatever reason unsuitable, the fee earner will refer it back to the provider, with a detailed request for the necessary improvement required to bring it into line with what was required.

In particular, any opinions or reports provided by the service provider should be carefully checked to ensure that they adequately provide the information sought and, in litigation matters, comply with the rules of court and any court orders.

If the standard of service or advice remains unsuitable, [name] will be consulted, and consideration will be given to the non-payment of the fee and the removal of the individual from the approved list of service providers.

The failure of the service provider to meet the practice's expectations must be recorded [*insert where this will be recorded. It could be on evaluation forms that are used by the practice or an electronic record of service providers*].

Recording and evaluation

The practice maintains a record of:

(a)   the use; and
(b)   evaluations of the performances of external service providers.

- [*insert details of where and how these records are kept;*
- *If the practice has a paper evaluation form, indicate a reference to the form.*]

[*N.B. The following paragraph represents an optional addition to the procedure for recording and evaluating the performances of external service providers. Each practice must decide whether this is appropriate for its particular approach to the subject.*]

[The practice has a system of grading external service providers: A, B, or C. Under normal circumstances, the first choice of provider will be made from someone in the A category, because these individuals normally meet the majority of the selection criteria that the practice uses. However, if that is not possible, a provider from the B category can be used, because providers within this category have normally been found to give a satisfactory service. Any provider within the C category will not normally be used, the reasons for which will be explained to fee earners by the individual who is recorded in the central record as having knowledge of the particular C category provider.]

It is likely that, from time to time, the practice will use several barristers from one set of chambers. When this is the case, evaluations will be undertaken of each individual barrister rather than a blanket evaluation of the chambers; the latter being insufficient.

In the circumstances where a service provider is regularly instructed by the practice, there is no need to evaluate their performance on every occasion that they are used, providing that their performance matches their original evaluation. Should a regularly instructed service provider fail to meet their usual standard of service, this must be recorded as described in (b) above.

It is most important that evaluations of performances are kept up to date and held centrally, in order that all members of the practice have access to them.

Payment of fees

[*Describe the practice's procedure for paying external service providers.*]

Review

The operation of this procedure will be reviewed by [*name*] at least annually, normally as part of the annual review of the office manual.

Annex 8D

File closure form

To be completed by the fee earner prior to archiving file.

Matter No:

Client:

N.B. If any of questions 1, 5, 6, 7, 8, 10, 12, 13, 14 and 15 are answered 'No', an explanation must be provided in the 'additional information' column.

No.	Checklist	Answer		Additional information
1.	Has all necessary information been given to the client on the outcome of the case?	Yes No	☐ ☐	
2.	Has all necessary information been given to the client on further action required on his/her/their part?	Yes No No requirement	☐ ☐ ☐	
3.	Has all necessary information been given to the client on what (if anything) the practice will do?	Yes No No requirement	☐ ☐ ☐	
4.	Is any after care action required?	Yes No	☐ ☐	
5.	Has the file been thinned and all unnecessary drafts/copies removed?	Yes No	☐ ☐	
6.	Has the client had all original documents/papers/property returned as required (save for items which by agreement are to be stored by the practice)?	Yes No Nothing to return	☐ ☐ ☐	
7.	Have all deeds/wills/documents been removed from the file and properly archived?	Yes No None held	☐ ☐ ☐	

8.	Have all bills been rendered and money accounted for to the client (including any interest due)?	Yes	☐	
		No	☐	
		No transactions	☐	
9.	Are there any outstanding balances?	Yes	☐	
		No	☐	
10.	Has the client been advised re the storage, retrieval and retention of papers and other items and any charges to be made in this respect?	Yes	☐	
		No	☐	
		No requirement	☐	
11.	Has the client been advised whether he/she/they should review the matter in the future?	Yes	☐	
		No	☐	
		Not necessary	☐	
		[If Yes, please provide date and why.]		
12.	Have all undertakings been complied with?	Yes	☐	
		No	☐	
		None	☐	
13.	Concluding risk assessment been carried out?	Yes	☐	
		No	☐	
14.	Have the client's objectives been met?	Yes	☐	
		No	☐	
		[If No, and the client could fairly complain or make a claim for damages in relation to the service provided, inform the head of department (HoD) and practice/risk manager immediately in writing giving full details.]		
15.	If the risk differs from the initial assessment, has the HoD/compliance director/risk manager been informed?	Yes	☐	
		No	☐	
		Risk unchanged	☐	

16.	Comments re final risk:
17.	Additional comments:

Fee earner signature:

Date: